CHRONOLOGIA

CHRONOLOGIA
HISTORY BY THE MINUTE

NORMAN FERGUSON

The History Press

For MCK & CFF – 9.38

Cover images (clockwise from top left):

Rear Admiral Sir Horatio Nelson. (National Maritme Museum/Public Domain)

The *Hindenburg* bursts into flames. (National Archives)

Man lands on the moon. (NASA)

The Great Fire of London. (Public Domain)

First published 2012

The History Press
The Mill, Brimscombe Port
Stroud, Gloucestershire, GL5 2QG
www.thehistorypress.co.uk

British Library Cataloguing in Publication Data.
A catalogue record for this book is available from the British Library.

ISBN 978 0 7524 7020 7

Typesetting and origination by The History Press
Printed in Great Britain

CONTENTS

INTRODUCTION

On 11 November 1918, the First World War was due to end. The armistice, signed earlier that morning, indicated that the four-year war was to finish at exactly 11.00 a.m. Fighting continued up until that time, and one man was shot and killed in the last minute of the war. As Private Henry Gunther advanced on a German machine-gun post, he was waved back by the German soldiers, who were desperate to avoid one more death so close to peace. Gunther continued and they were left with no option but to fire. He died at 10.59 a.m. and it was reported that the rest of the guns on the whole front fell silent almost immediately after.

The fact that one aspect of the conflict – the futile deaths of so many on the Western Front – could be defined in one specific moment in time, served as an inspiration for this book. We are accustomed to history being arranged by era, century, decade, year or specific dates. *Chronologia* takes a different approach, arranging events by the time of day. It includes around 400 moments of history, sport and culture, going as far back as 55 BC.

Human history is as chaotic and random as human life, and this book attempts to reflect some of that.

Norman Ferguson
8.12 a.m.
2 November 2011

NOTES

Note on the Times

Where possible, all times included are 'local' from where the event took place. Where it has proved impossible to pin down the time zone in use, GMT is used. Space missions are entered using GMT, apart from launches and Earth landings, which follow the convention of following the time in the location involved. For example, NASA missions use Eastern Daylight/Summer Time as their flights were launched from Florida.

Note on Accuracy

The author has tried to be as accurate as possible, both in terms of the description of events and when they happened. Where he has failed, lay the failure on him. As with all human endeavours errors will inevitably creep in. If any are spotted the author would be grateful to hear about them at chronologiahistory@gmail.com.

Standardisation

In the interests of commonality all times are presented in a standard format. Of course some events could never be recorded to the exact minute, especially the further back in time you go, but they are presented here in a standard way for ease of reading.

ACKNOWLEDGEMENTS

Researching the information for *Chronologia* was appropriately a time-consuming task. It would have been impossible but for the resources of the following main sources: BBC, *The Times*, the *Guardian*, Eyewitnesstohistory.com, history.com, NASA.

MIDNIGHT TO 12.59 A.M.

12.00 a.m.

A fleet of ships sets sail from northern France. They are heading for Britain under the command of a Roman governor of Gaul called Julius Caesar. Caesar's forces land near Deal in Kent and, despite ferocious attacks by the Britons, are able to maintain a foothold. However, when his cavalry are unable to land, Caesar orders a retreat back across the English Channel. He makes another attempt the following year but the Romans do not establish a dominating presence in Britannia until 100 years later. During their occupation, they encounter the rebellion under Boudicca and are forced to build a wall that forms the northernmost boundary to their empire.

(23 August 55 BC)

12.00 a.m.

Sir Thomas Knyvett searches the cellar underneath London's Palace of Westminster and discovers thirty-six barrels of gunpowder. He also finds a man claiming to be John Johnson, who is in fact Guy Fawkes, one of a band of English Catholic conspirators planning to blow up Parliament and kill King James VI and I. Fawkes is tortured and confesses to committing treason. He escapes the horrors of being hanged, drawn and quartered by jumping off the scaffold and hanging himself. Despite this, the punishment is still carried out on his corpse. Bonfires are lit to celebrate the survival of the king.

(Tuesday 5 November 1605)

12.01 a.m.

The first baby is born under Britain's new National Health Service. Aneira Thomas is named after Minister for Health Aneurin Bevan who, on the same day, accepts the keys to Park Hospital in Manchester as a symbolic start to a scheme free and available to all citizens. The NHS forms part of new social security measures including sickness and unemployment benefit and better pensions for those who have paid National Insurance. Child benefit is brought in, as is income support for the needy. Labour Prime Minister Clement Attlee described it as: 'the most comprehensive system of social security ever introduced into any country.' Aneira Thomas goes on to become a nurse.

(Monday 5 July 1948)

12.01 a.m.

Millions of computer users relax when they find the threatened 'Millennium Bug' has not struck. The potential problem is a result of computer programmes only using two digits for year dates. Whether machines and vehicles would continue to work after midnight occupies much discussion and re-engineering beforehand. No major systems are affected and no planes fall out of the sky.

(Saturday 1 January 2000)

12.01 a.m.

Bookshops open to sell *Harry Potter and the Deathly Hallows*, the last novel in the popular series. It becomes the fastest-selling book of all time with 2.7 million copies sold in the UK in 24 hours. J.K. Rowling's series of seven adventures featuring Hermione, Ron and the troubled boy wizard Harry, has sold over 450 million copies and inspired untold numbers of young readers.

(Saturday 21 July 2007)

12.04 a.m.

Oil supertanker *Exxon Valdez* runs aground in Alaska. Eight of the ship's eleven oil tanks are breached. The spill is the largest the United States has ever seen, with 1,300 miles of coastline affected by 11 million gallons of crude oil. Crew negligence is found to be the cause.

(Friday 24 March 1989)

12.10 a.m.

The first of the trapped Chilean miners is rescued. Florencio Avalos is slowly pulled up through a 2,300ft-long narrow tunnel specially drilled to take the 'Phoenix' capsule. Avalos is the first of the thirty-three men trapped underground to be brought to the surface. The miners have spent ten weeks in the San Jose copper and gold mine in northern Chile. Their story of endurance captures the imagination of a watching world.

(Wednesday 13 October 2010)

12.10 a.m.

Lieutenant Colonel Claus von Stauffenberg is shot by firing squad. Along with other conspirators he has been executed for his role in an unsuccessful coup that depended on the death of Adolf Hitler. The day before, von Stauffenberg had placed a bomb hidden in a briefcase under a conference table near to the Führer. The bomb detonated but only wounded Hitler. The plot was an attempt to install a new government that would have negotiated an armistice with the Allies in order to prevent the Russians from entering Germany. Some of the conspirators commit suicide, while others are killed in barbarous ways.

(Friday 21 July 1944)

12.10 a.m.

Ten minutes late, Big Ben chimes to bring in the New Year 1963. Snow has affected the clock's hands, slowing the mechanism. Since its construction in 1858, London's landmark clock has been slowed, silenced or stopped by maintenance, heat, birds, war and metal fatigue. Although the whole tower is known as 'Big Ben' the nickname was intended only for the 13-ton bell.

(Tuesday 1 January 1963)

12.10 a.m.

East Sussex police are called to Brian Jones' house. The musician, who had been sacked from rock group the Rolling Stones just days before, is found at the bottom of a swimming pool. Whether Jones died by accident or was murdered remains a topic for discussion years afterwards.

(Thursday 3 July 1969)

12.14 a.m.

Torpedoes hit the USS *Indianapolis*. The US Navy ship is returning from dropping off uranium for the Hiroshima atomic bomb when it is seen by chance by a Japanese submarine. With not enough time to launch sufficient life rafts, the sailors have only their life jackets for buoyancy. They suffer dehydration, exposure and attacks by sharks for five days. Out of the 1,197 sailors and marines on board, only 317 survive. Captain McVay is the only US Navy captain to be court martialled for losing his ship. Although cleared, he is found dead in 1968, his death caused by self-inflicted gunshot wounds.

(Monday 30 July 1945)

12.15 a.m.

Gas starts to leak from a pesticide plant in Bhopal, India. The cloud of toxic methyl isocyanate is blown across the local area and several thousand are killed immediately with more dying in the following years. The Indian government estimates that 500,000 people have suffered injuries from exposure to the gas. The owners of the factory, the American company Union Carbide, attempt to avoid responsibility and when they do pay compensation it is viewed as being insufficient for such a devastating tragedy. Bhopal becomes a byword for corporate negligence.

(Monday 3 December 1984)

12.15 a.m.

A 42-year-old Austrian woman called Elisabeth Fritzl finishes giving a statement to police. On the promise that she never has to see her father again, she tells police about her twenty-four years of incarceration in a small cellar under the family home. She reveals that she has been raped around 3,000 times by her father Joseph Fritzl, and had seven children by him, one of whom died as Fritzl wouldn't seek medical help. He is tried and sentenced to life imprisonment for his crimes. The director of intensive medicine at the hospital says of Elisabeth: 'I have rarely seen such a strong woman.'

(Sunday 27 April 2008)

12.20 a.m.

A Mercedes limousine carrying Diana, Princess of Wales, and her partner Dodi Fayed, crashes into a pillar in a Parisian underpass. The 65mph smash kills Diana, Fayed and the driver Henri Paul, who is later found to be over the legal drink-driving alcohol limit. Diana's bodyguard Trevor Rees-Jones survives but his memory of the incident is impaired. The Princess of Wales's death provokes unprecedented scenes of national mourning.

(Sunday 31 August 1997)

12.28 a.m.

The first bouncing bomb of the Dambusters raid is dropped. Wing Commander Guy Gibson's Lancaster begins the low-level attack on Germany's Ruhr dams using this unique weapon. The raid is costly: eight of 617 Squadron's nineteen planes do not return and fifty-three of its men are killed. Over 1,300 German civilians, foreign labourers and Allied prisoners of war also die. While the mission is an operational success, its chief achievement is in its propaganda value.

(Monday 17 May 1943)

12.28 a.m.: First bomb is dropped in the Dambusters raid. (Arpingstone)

12.30 a.m.

The first of Captain Scott's men dies in the Antarctic. Seaman Edgar Evans has been suffering from concussion and may have had a nervous breakdown. Returning from the disheartening discovery that they have been beaten to the South Pole by the Norwegians, Scott and four others are in the middle of facing the '800 miles of solid dragging' that Scott described as lying ahead of them on their return. The British party have already been walking back from the Pole for a month when Evans dies, and continue for another month before being stopped by bad weather. In their last camp, on 29 March, Scott writes in his diary: 'I do not think we can hope for any better things now. We shall stick it out to the end, but we are getting weaker, of course, and the end cannot be far. It seems a pity, but I do not think I can write more.'

(Sunday 18 February 1912)

12.30 a.m.

Rasputin leaves his St Petersburg apartment for an assignation with the wife of Prince Felix Yussupov. It is a ruse by the prince and other conspirators to get the 'Mad Monk' to a place where they hope to poison him. The attempt fails and in desperation Rasputin is beaten, shot and eventually dumped into the Neva River. Russians have become alarmed at the effect the ex-peasant has had on the country and the reputation of the monarchy. There are later claims that because Rasputin favoured withdrawing Russian troops from the fight against Germany and thereby increasing the amount of German soldiers to fight on the Western Front, a British Secret Service agent fires the fatal last shot.

(Saturday 17 December 1917)

12.44 a.m.

Timothy Leary dies of cancer. His exhortation to 'Turn On, Tune In and Drop Out' had been the clarion call for the psychedelic sixties. His advocation of expanding consciousness through the use of illegal drugs made him the target of federal authorities. President Nixon called Leary 'the most dangerous man in America'. In 1973, the ex-Harvard lecturer is recaptured following a jail escape. He finds Charles Manson in a neighbouring cell. Manson tells him: 'I've been waiting to talk to you for years.'

(Friday 31 May 1996)

12.45 a.m.

Joe Simpson reaches base camp. He is met by his climbing partner Simon Yates who cannot believe that Simpson is alive. The two had made the first ascent of the western face of the 21,000ft Peruvian Andes mountain Siula Grande but had run into difficulties on their descent. Simpson had fallen and shattered his leg and then had become stuck, suspended over a crevasse. Yates cut Simpson's rope to save himself before making his own way off the mountain. Simpson falls 150ft into the crevasse and then crawls for three and a half days, dehydrated and in abject agony. When he reaches help he is near to death. Their experiences are related in the book and film *Touching the Void.*

(Tuesday 11 June 1985)

12.50 a.m.

After being chased through the streets of Los Angeles by police, Rodney King stops his car. He is subjected to a heavy beating by police officers. The incident is videotaped by a bystander and when the footage is shown on television it becomes a major story. The officers' acquittal triggers riots that lead to fifty-three people being killed in Los Angeles. Two of the officers are later found guilty at a federal trial and King wins $3.8 million in damages.

(Sunday 3 March 1991)

12.55 a.m.

A light aircraft takes off from Mason City Municipal Airport in Iowa. On board are musicians Buddy Holly, Ritchie Valens and 'The Big Bopper' Jiles P. Richardson. The flight only lasts a few minutes, as the plane crashes into a field. All on board are killed. Buddy Holly only released three albums before his death but has had a huge influence on popular music. Singer-songwriter Don McLean later sang of this event as 'the day the music died'.

(Tuesday 3 February 1959)

1.00 A.M. TO 1.59 A.M.

1.00 a.m.

A fire breaks out in a bakery in London's Pudding Lane. It spreads and destroys eight tenths of the city within days. Despite the scale of the inferno, loss of life from the Great Fire of London is remarkably low. One positive benefit is the eradication of the plague that had been in the city since 1665, as the fire kills most of the rat population. London is rebuilt and one of its iconic landmarks is created: the new St Paul's Cathedral. Designed by Christopher Wren, the cathedral survives another inferno in the Blitz of the Second World War.

(Sunday 2 September 1666)

1.00 a.m.

A resident of Abbottabad in Pakistan reports on social networking site Twitter that he can hear a helicopter. The helicopter is carrying American Special Forces soldiers, who enter a house inside a walled compound in the town. They find and shoot dead Osama Bin Laden, the leader of Islamic terrorist group Al-Qaeda.

(Monday 2 May 2011)

1.17 a.m.

Bobby Sands dies. The IRA prisoner has been on hunger strike for sixty-six days inside Belfast's Maze prison. Nine more Irish republican hunger strikers follow him to their deaths. Their protests are aimed at improving conditions inside the prison. After the crisis is over, some of their demands are granted by the British government. Sands had been jailed for possession of a firearm used in a gunfight with Northern Ireland's police force.

(Tuesday 5 May 1981)

1.00 a.m.: The Great Fire of London begins. (Yale Center for British Art)

1.20 a.m.

The Met Office issues a severe weather warning. Winds that were forecast to be 'fresh to strong' have reached storm force 11. The Great Storm of 1987 causes widespread devastation across the south-east of England. It damages thousands of buildings, flattens 15 million trees, capsizes a bulk carrier, and forces a cross-Channel ferry aground. Fatalities are relatively low for such a ferocious storm, with fewer than twenty killed in the UK. Forecasters, Michael Fish in particular, receive much criticism for not predicting the strength of the storm.

(Friday 16 October 1987)

1.24 a.m.

The Chernobyl nuclear plant in Ukraine suffers a catastrophic explosion. During a test the nuclear reactor overheats and causes a blast that tears the roof open. The breach allows radioactive material to escape, some of which lands on the surrounding local area in the form of lumps of graphite. A large radioactive cloud is blown westwards and spreads over most of Europe. The radioactivity released is 400 times that of Hiroshima. The nearby town of Pripyat is evacuated and remains uninhabited to the present day.

(Saturday 26 April 1986)

1.30 a.m.

Radio Prague broadcasts news that foreign troops and tanks have entered Czechoslovakia. An appeal goes out to the wider world: 'We are with you, be with us'. The Russians, along with Polish, Bulgarian, East German and Hungarian soldiers, are there to quell the Prague Spring. Czech leader Alexander Dubček has instigated liberal reforms that Moscow views as potentially damaging to the security of the Soviet Union and the Warsaw Pact. Dubček urges Czechs not to oppose the invasion, but around 100 civilians are killed. Dubček is allowed to remain in power, but is replaced the following year. He returns to national politics in 1989 following the Velvet Revolution.

(Wednesday 21 August 1968)

1.30 a.m.

Actor Hugh Grant and prostitute Divine Brown are arrested by Los Angeles police. Grant had picked up Brown on Los Angeles' Sunset Boulevard and 20 minutes later they were interrupted by police officers. Grant is fined and placed on probation but is given credit for publicly facing up to his indiscretion. Brown takes advantage of her newfound fame and earns enough to give her daughters private school education.

(Tuesday 27 June 1995)

1.44 a.m.

Senator Robert F. Kennedy dies after being shot in the kitchen of a Los Angeles hotel. He was leaving the hotel following a victory speech given after his success in the Californian Democratic primary for the US presidential elections. Robert had three brothers, only one of whom – Edward – lived to see old age. His oldest brother Joseph was killed in the Second World War and his brother John was assassinated while president.

(Thursday 6 June 1968)

1.45 a.m.

The Canadian Olympic Team leader, Carol Anne Letheren, is woken to be told that sprinter Ben Johnson has tested positive for steroids. His run in the 100m final two days previously was an electrifying 9.79 seconds, a time that smashed the world record and saw Johnson slowing up near the end. He crossed the finish line doing 27mph. Following the revelation, he is sent home in disgrace and is stripped of his Olympic title. When asked beforehand what meant more, the medal or the record, Johnson said: 'The medal. It is something that no one can take away from you'.

(Monday 26 September 1988)

1.46 a.m.

The *Marchioness* pleasure boat, hosting a twenty-sixth birthday party with 132 people on board, collides with the gravel dredger *Bowbelle* on the River Thames. The *Marchioness*, which had rescued British troops from Dunkirk in 1940, sinks within 30 seconds. Fifty-one people drown.

(Sunday 20 August 1989)

1.57 a.m.

RAF bombers leave the skies over the German city of Dresden. Over 2,500 tons of high explosives and incendiary bombs have been dropped. The resulting devastation, costing the lives of around 25,000 people, is held as a sign of needless destruction, with the Second World War almost won. Others view the bombing of Dresden as no different from other bombing raids carried out in Europe and Asia in an effort to end the war more quickly.

(Wednesday 14 February 1945)

2.00 A.M. TO 2.59 A.M.

2.00 a.m.

A sailor on the *Pinta*, one of three ships under the command of Christopher Columbus, sights land. The Italian explorer had set sail from Spain ten weeks earlier to discover the riches of the east, but instead reaches the Bahamas. The Europeans think they have reached the Indies and so call the inhabitants Indians. Columbus makes three more transatlantic journeys that start the process of European colonial expansion. He is rewarded by being made Governor of the Indies, but is later punished for meting out harsh punishments on the Spanish settlers.

(Friday 12 October 1492)

2.00 a.m.: Christopher Columbus crosses the Atlantic. (L. Prang & Co.)

2.00 a.m.

Mary, Queen of Scots, writes her last letter, to her brother-in-law King Henry III of France. She is to be executed in 6 hours' time on the orders of her cousin, Queen Elizabeth I of England. Mary had returned to Scotland from France in 1561 to become queen, but her designs on the English throne lead to her ultimate downfall. On the scaffold she said to her executioner: 'I forgive you with all my heart, for now, I hope, you shall make an end of all my troubles'. She becomes a symbol of religious martyrdom and a tragic figure of history.

(Wednesday 8 February 1587)

2.00 a.m.

Petrograd's Winter Palace is taken as part of Russia's October Revolution. Although later portrayed as an epic battle, very little resistance is offered by the meagre defending forces. The Winter Palace becomes the seat of the provisional government that is set up after the fall of the tsar. Civil war ensues until the Bolsheviks under Lenin are victorious and set up a Communist state.

(Thursday 25 October 1917)

2.00 a.m.

German businessman Otto Frank sees his family for the last time. Frank, his wife Edith and daughters Anne and Margot, have lived above his company's premises in Amsterdam for two years. Their secret annex has been betrayed to the authorities and they are transported by rail to Auschwitz concentration camp. Of their arrival at the camp he later says: 'I shall remember the look in Margot's eyes all my life.' Otto Frank is the only member of his family to survive and later publishes his daughter Anne's diaries.

(Tuesday 5 September 1944)

2.00 a.m.

Visitors start queuing for the opening day of Disneyland: the world's first theme park. The Californian attraction receives 50,000 visitors on its first day and over 600 million in the next fifty years. The park is the first of several Disney attractions to be built around the world. Despite

'Mickey Mouse' often being used as a derogatory term, Disney is the most successful media conglomerate in the world.

(Monday 18 July 1955)

2.00 a.m.

In the middle of the Iranian desert a US Marine helicopter crashes into a US Air Force Hercules cargo aircraft. They are part of a risky military mission ordered by President Carter to rescue fifty-three American hostages from Tehran. Operation Eagle Claw is being aborted when the collision occurs. Eight men are killed. The Tehran hostages are later released on the day that President Ronald Reagan is inaugurated.

(Friday 25 April 1980)

2.00 a.m.

American aircraft bomb Libya. One of the targets is a compound where the Libyan leader Colonel Gaddafi is believed to be staying. He escapes the bombs, and it is later revealed that he was given advance warning of the raid by an Italian politician. The US planes have flown from Britain to carry out the attack, which is in response to terrorist attacks on US citizens. Two years later Pan American flight 103 is blown up over Scotland and in 2001 a Libyan intelligence officer is found guilty of planting the bomb.

(Tuesday 15 April 1986)

2.00 a.m.

Iraq invades Kuwait. The Kuwaitis put up spirited resistance but their outnumbered armed forces are quickly defeated. With the backing of the United Nations, a coalition of US-led armed forces prepare to expel the Iraqi occupying army. The resulting Gulf War in January and February 1991 sees the Iraq Army defeated and the Kuwaiti government restored.

(Thursday 2 August 1990)

2.25 a.m.

Tiger Woods' SUV hits a tree and comes to a halt. The golfer is found lying on the road with his wife Elin Nordegren next to him. Both rear windows of his Cadillac Escalade have been smashed in with a golf club. Days before, a newspaper had printed allegations of Woods' infidelity. Following the car crash, more revelations about his sex life are revealed. His divorce costs the richest-ever athlete millions in cancelled endorsement contracts and a reputed $100 million settlement with his ex-wife.

(Friday 27 November 2009)

2.30 a.m.

Workers at the Homestead steel plant sound the alarm when they see barges containing Pinkerton agents approaching. The Pinkerton security men have been hired by the plant's owners, the Carnegie Steel Company, to ensure that non-unionised workers can enter the plant. A conflict starts that sees ten people killed: seven workers and three Pinkerton men. The incident is one of the worst in American industrial relations. Andrew Carnegie, whose entrepreneurial efforts make him a rich man, later sells the company for $480 million and devotes the latter part of his life to philanthropy such as funding libraries, colleges, schools and trusts.

(Wednesday 6 July 1892)

2.30 a.m.

Berlin is divided. The East German government seals the border between East and West Berlin to stop the westerly emigration of the working population. Before the border is closed 1,500 people were leaving East Berlin each week. Desperate East Berliners use various methods to try and escape, including sneaking through unsafe, bombed buildings and swimming across rivers and canals. An East German soldier joins the escapees he is meant to be stopping by leaping over barbed wire. Border guards shoot over 200 escapees before the wall comes down almost thirty years later.

(Sunday 13 August 1961)

2.30 a.m.

Five men are arrested at the Watergate office and hotel complex in Washington DC. They have been involved in a burglary at offices used by the Democratic Party. The Watergate scandal leads to the resignation of President Nixon who defends himself by saying: 'I am not a crook.' He is later pardoned by his successor Gerald Ford. The investigation into the scandal is aided by a secret informant known as 'Deep Throat' who guides two reporters, Bob Woodward and Carl Bernstein, towards the truth. After much speculation the informant is revealed to be a senior FBI official.

(Saturday 17 June 1972)

2.30 a.m.

Al Gore telephones George W. Bush to concede the 2000 presidential election. An hour later he calls back to take back his concession following media retractions of earlier predictions of a Bush victory. The confusion centres over a very close vote in Florida, which leads to a month of legal wrangling. Eventually the Supreme Court decides in favour of the Republican Bush and Gore finally concedes defeat. Bush goes on to serve two terms as president while Gore, who secured 500,000 more votes in the election, becomes an environmental campaigner.

(Wednesday 8 November 2000)

2.51 a.m.

The *Beagle 2* is scheduled to enter the atmosphere of the planet Mars. The British-designed and built lander had been released from its mothership *Mars Express Orbiter* six days previously, following a 250 million-mile journey from Earth. If it had landed successfully, *Beagle 2* would have played a nine-note tune by British band Blur. No signal is received following its release.

(Thursday 25 December 2003)

2.54 a.m.

A bomb planted by the IRA explodes in Brighton's Grand Hotel. The Conservative Party are holding their annual conference in the town and senior figures in the government, including Prime Minister Margaret Thatcher, are staying in the hotel. Five people are killed and over thirty are injured in the blast. The man convicted of the attack is later released following the Good Friday Agreement.

(Friday 12 October 1984)

3.00 A.M. TO 3.59 A.M.

3.00 a.m.

Good Queen Bess dies. The Elizabethan era has seen England increase its military power and start a process of colonisation across the world, particularly in America. The last Tudor monarch dies unmarried and without an heir, after being on the throne for forty-four years. In a matter of hours her successor is proclaimed: the Protestant Scottish King James VI, who makes his way south from Edinburgh within weeks. When he is crowned James I of England, the crowns of England and Scotland are united in one person for the first time.

(Thursday 24 March 1603)

3.00 a.m.

The 'Great Storm of 1703' reaches its peak over the south-east of England, with hurricane-force winds leaving a trail of destruction. An estimated 8,000 people die, including 1,000 Royal Navy sailors who are lost when their ships are sunk or battered by the winds. Thousands of buildings are damaged, with many churches losing their spires. The Eddystone lighthouse is blown over, killing its builder Henry Winstanley. A woman killed when the chimneystack falls through the roof of her house is commemorated with a memorial slab that remembers the 'furious hurricane'. In a macabre incident, the recently exhumed head of Oliver Cromwell is blown off its spike.

(Saturday 27 November 1703)

3.00 a.m.

Grave robbers are discovered removing Dick Turpin's body from its grave. He had been buried two days previously after being hanged for horse theft. He had also carried out housebreaking, deer poaching, torture and murder, as well as the highway robberies he is remembered for. Writers romanticise Turpin's life heavily following his death.

(Tuesday 10 April 1739)

3.00 a.m.

In stormy conditions, the SS *Forfarshire* runs aground on the Ferne Islands off Northumberland. The nearby lighthouse keeper and his daughter, Grace Horsely Darling, row a small coble boat to the wreckage of the ship. They have to row a mile in gale-force winds to reach the stranded survivors. Nine are taken off to safety by the Darlings' boat. Grace becomes a national heroine for carrying out, as she described them, 'my humble endeavours'. She dies of tuberculosis four years later, her untimely death only adding to her iconic status.

(Friday 7 September 1838)

3.10 a.m.

Michael Portillo loses his seat. Portillo, the defence minister in the Conservative government, loses to Stephen Twigg of the Labour Party in the 1997 General Election. The shock result's announcement on television becomes a symbolic moment of the defeat of the Conservatives after eighteen years in power.

(Friday 2 May 1997)

3.14 a.m.

Reality TV star Jade Goody dies. Essex-born Goody came to prominence during her appearance on Channel 4's *Big Brother*. She became a regular feature of celebrity columns and magazines. Goody was appearing in a *Big Brother* show in India when told she had cervical cancer. She said: 'I've lived in front of the cameras. And maybe I'll die in front of them.' She dies on Mother's Day.

(Sunday 22 March 2009)

3.15 a.m.

The mail train to London from Glasgow is halted by a signal in Buckinghamshire and thieves get away with £2.6 million in what becomes known as the 'Great Train Robbery'. Jack Mills, the driver of the train, is injured by the robbers, most of whom are later arrested and jailed. One of those convicted, Ronnie Biggs, becomes a celebrity while on the run. He returns to Britain in 2001 an ill man and is jailed on his return.

(Thursday 8 August 1963)

3.24 a.m.

American inventor Thomas Edison dies. Edison holds over 1,000 patents and among his inventions are the first commercially viable incandescent light bulb, the phonograph, alkaline batteries and a means of projecting moving images. Edison's ability to innovate, coupled with a conscious desire to only produce devices that would be sellable, made him a wealthy man. In relation to his working methods, which involved careful deduction, he famously said: 'Genius is 1 per cent inspiration and 99 per cent perspiration.'

(Sunday 18 October 1931)

3.26 a.m.

A Korean airliner is fired on by a Soviet fighter aircraft. The Boeing 747 is heading to Seoul from the United States when two air-to-air missiles are launched, disabling the airliner's controls. The plane has accidentally drifted off course and entered Russian airspace. All 269 on board are killed and the event causes a major Cold War incident.

(Thursday 1 September 1983)

3.30 a.m.

Martin Luther King finishes writing a speech he will give later that day. His 'I Have a Dream' oration inspires the 200,000 civil rights marchers who are in Washington and those watching live on television. King is awarded the Nobel Peace Prize the following year.

(Wednesday 28 August 1963)

3.38 a.m.

A telegram is handed in at a Cairo station. It is addressed to Mrs Eleanor Philby, who lives in Beirut, and reads: 'All going well … letters with all details following soon … Kim Philby.' Kim Philby had left Beiruit suddenly

3.30 a.m.: Martin Luther King. (Phil Stanziola, Library of Congress, *New York World/Telegram & Sun* Collection)

in January. His wife claimed that he had gone on special assignment for the *Observer* or *The Economist* but neither paper had knowledge of his whereabouts. Philby doesn't return to Beirut but heads to Moscow where he remains for the rest of his life. He is the 'Third Man', one of a group of spies who had given British secrets to the Soviet Union since the Second World War. Philby's wife visits him in Moscow but they divorce after Philby has an affair with another spy's wife.

(Saturday 2 March 1963)

3.45 a.m.

A police constable in Whitechapel, London, finds a woman lying on the street. At first he thinks she is drunk, but on closer inspection finds that her throat has been cut. She is Mary Ann Nicholls, the first victim of a serial killer known as 'Jack the Ripper' (also 'The Whitechapel Murderer' and 'Leather Apron'), who kills at least four and possibly eight women in London's East End. His nickname stems from the gruesome nature of the killings: some of the dead have internal organs cut out. Despite the intense interest of the police, media and the public, Jack the Ripper is never brought to justice.

(Friday 31 August 1888)

4.00 A.M. TO 4.59 A.M.

4.00 a.m.

Swedish pop group ABBA's celebrations end after their win in the Eurovision Song Contest. The foursome of Benny Andersson, Agnetha Fältstkog, Björn Ulvaeus and Anni-Frid Lyngstad win the contest with the song 'Waterloo', which becomes a number one in several countries. Andersson had placed a £100 bet at odds of 12 to 1 on his group winning. As one of the songwriters, he goes on to earn as much as £100 million from the group's worldwide success.

(Sunday 7 April 1974)

4.00 a.m.

A reactor unit at the Three Mile Island nuclear plant in Dauphin County, Pennsylvania, starts to overheat. Plant workers fail to react properly and the nuclear core heats to 4,000 degrees, nearly causing a catastrophic meltdown. A few days later the State Governor of Pennsylvania orders a partial evacuation but this leads to panic. The meltdown is avoided but faith in nuclear power is diminished and America does not build any more atomic power stations.

(Wednesday 28 March 1979)

4.00 a.m.

The streetlights around Beijing's Tiananmen Square are switched off as Chinese troops and tanks quash a democracy protest. Despite international condemnation, the Chinese government continues its crackdown on democracy supporters. An image of a lone protestor attempting to halt a tank's progress becomes the symbolic image of the event. The final death toll is not known.

(Sunday 4 June 1989)

4.15 a.m.: D-Day landings, 1944. (Robert F. Sargent, USCG)

4.15 a.m.

After abandoning their rubber dinghies to swim the rest of the way, four American soldiers reach two small islands off the Normandy coast. Armed only with knives, they are the first seaborne Allied troops to land on French soil. The Îles Saint-Marcouf are secured and the way is cleared for the amphibious landing on Utah Beach a few hours later. It is one of five beaches where over 130,000 US, Canadian, British and other Allied troops land in the first day of the campaign to liberate Europe.

(Tuesday 6 June 1944)

4.15 a.m.

British Royal Marines exit their landing craft and move onto the beaches at Port Said. The Egyptian town is on the Suez Canal, which has been brought under Egyptian state control by President Nasser. France and Britain – who had controlled the canal since its construction in 1869 – devise a secret plan with Israel. French and British forces are sent in with the stated aims of restoring peace following Israeli military action. The watching world is not fooled by this deception plan and international criticism mounts. British Prime Minister Anthony Eden backs down and orders a ceasefire. The humiliating end to the crisis is seen as the end of Britain's world-power status.

(Tuesday 6 November 1956)

4.25 a.m.

Marilyn Monroe's doctors telephone Los Angeles Police to report her death. The coroner records that the Hollywood star died of 'probable suicide' although alternative theories involving President Kennedy and his brother Robert continue to circulate. Whatever the cause of death, the movie world loses one of its biggest stars.

(Sunday 5 August 1962)

4.25 a.m.

Robert Maxwell is last seen alive when the captain of his luxury yacht sees him at the ship's stern. The newspaper tycoon's body is later found in the sea off Tenerife. Whether through accident, suicide, or murder, Maxwell's death is not explained. It is discovered later that he had raided his companies' pension funds to shore up his other failing businesses.

(Tuesday 5 November 1991)

4.30 a.m.

Cannons open fire on Fort Sumter in the opening shots of the American Civil War. The island fort guards Charleston Harbor in South Carolina, and is being attacked by Confederate forces who force the fort's surrender the next day. Despite the bombardment, no soldier is killed or injured. In the ensuing four years of war, fought over the South's desire to secede from the Union, over 600,000 are killed through combat injuries or disease. Thirty per cent of all males from the South aged 18–40 die in the conflict.

(Friday 12 April 1861)

4.30 a.m.

Mrs Lucy Esposito awakes and tends to her daughter Elaine. Elaine is in the final day of a coma that has lasted 37 years and 111 days – the longest time anyone has remained in that condition. Aged 6, she went into hospital in August 1941 for an appendectomy and never awoke. Mrs Esposito had always hoped Elaine would die first, so that her daughter would always have someone to look after her.

(Sunday 26 November 1978)

4.30 a.m.

Jayne Torvill and Christopher Dean are up early for practice at Sarajevo's Zetra Ice Stadium. Later that day they perform to Ravel's 'Bolero' in the Winter Olympics pairs ice dancing final. They are awarded perfect scores for artistic impression by all nine judges. Twenty-four million Britons watch the gold-medal-winning 4.5-minute performance.

(Tuesday 14 February 1984)

4.30 a.m.

Palestinian terrorists climb a fence into the Olympic Village in Munich. They take members of the Israeli team hostage, killing two immediately. Their aims are to secure the release of over 200 prisoners. The German police attempt a rescue attempt but the terrorists see them preparing their assault on live television. The Palestinians and their hostages are taken to a German airfield where the inadequately prepared police open fire. During the gunfight a grenade is thrown into one of the helicopters. All nine hostages are killed, plus a German policeman and five of the terrorists. Three of the captured terrorists are later released.

(Tuesday 5 September 1972)

4.30 a.m.

Heathrow Airport's brand new Terminal 5 sees its first passenger go through security. While his flight departs successfully, others are cancelled in an event that MPs later describe as a 'national embarrassment'. Chaos ensues as the £4.3 billion terminal's newly installed baggage system fails to operate successfully. In the first five days, 500 flights are cancelled.

(Thursday 27 March 2008)

4.35 a.m.

Louis Blériot takes off from near Calais. The Frenchman intends to become the first to fly the English Channel. His monoplane carries him at a speed of around 40mph, only a few hundred feet above the sea. For 10 minutes he flies without reference to either coast. He finally sees the English coast but realises he is off course and picks a landing spot near Dover. His journey has taken less than 40 minutes, long enough to make Blériot internationally famous.

(Sunday 25 July 1909)

5.00 A.M. TO 5.59 A.M.

5.00 a.m.

A party that has gone ashore from the *Mayflower* awake shortly before being attacked by Indians – just one of the hazards they have faced since arriving at Cape Cod. The 'Pilgrim Fathers' have travelled from England to find new lives, hoping to enjoy better religious freedom. Half of them die in the first winter from diseases such as scurvy and tuberculosis. Despite the obstacles, they are able to establish the first permanent settlement in 'New England'.

(Friday 8 December 1620)

5.00 a.m.

Government soldiers start the killing in one of the most notorious events in British history. The Massacre of Glencoe sees troops who have been staying with the MacDonald clan for a week and a half turn on their Highland hosts. King William has ordered a crackdown on unruly Jacobite clans, and by failing to make an oath of loyalty in time, the leader of the Glencoe MacDonalds gives the government an opportunity to make an example of them. Thirty-eight men, women and children are killed immediately with as many dying of exposure later. The government soldiers are led by Captain Robert Campbell and the clan Campbell earns a tainted reputation that persists hundreds of years later, despite evidence that they helped some of the MacDonalds to escape.

(Saturday 13 February 1692)

5.00 a.m.

British troops reach the Massachusetts town of Lexington. They are met by a small force of local militia. Shots are fired and eight American minutemen are killed. The American War of Independence from British colonial rule has begun. The following year, on 4 July, the Declaration of Independence is passed by Congress. The war, which sees Britain defeated by the combined forces of Spain, France and the Dutch Republic on the American side, ends in 1783.

(Wednesday 19 April 1775)

5.00 a.m.

Off Newfoundland, Edward Coward, the master of the brig *Renovation*, is called to see two ships that are stuck in the ice. Through his telescope he views their broken masts but sees no sign of the crews. It doesn't strike him until later that they may be the missing ships *Erebus* and *Terror* of Sir John Franklin's Arctic expedition. No news is heard from the missing expedition, and it is not until 1854 when John Rae of the Hudson Bay Company brings back expedition objects that any faint hopes are finally dashed. The situation is made worse when Rae also reports evidence of cannibalism among some emaciated survivors seen by the Inuit. This shocks Victorian society and Rae is ostracised for revealing it.

(Sunday 20 April 1851)

5.00 a.m.

George Orwell is shot. The writer had travelled to Spain to fight on the side of the Republicans in the Civil War and is at the front near Huesca when a single bullet passes through his throat. At first he thinks he will die but he recovers and returns to Britain where he continues writing. During the war Orwell serves in the Home Guard. His experiences of how the Stalinist Spanish Communist Party attacked the Workers' Party influences his writing, resulting in the anti-totalitarian *Animal Farm* and *Nineteen Eighty-Four.*

(Thursday 20 May 1937)

5.10 a.m.

The armistice that will end the First World War is signed. In a train carriage in a forest near Compiègne, the French commander Marshall Foch oversees the German acceptance of defeat. The armistice will come into effect at 11.00 a.m. later that morning. Twenty-two years later Hitler forces the French to surrender to him in the same carriage.

(Monday 11 November 1918)

5.10 a.m.: Armistice to end the First World War is signed. (Duhjeroen)

5.12 a.m.

Western America is shaken by a major earthquake of the San Andreas Fault. The shaking lasts up to a minute. San Francisco is near the epicentre and the tremor starts fires that devastate the city, causing almost 30,000 buildings to be lost. It is estimated that the quake and fire result in the deaths of 3,000 people.

(Wednesday 18 April 1906)

5.28 a.m.

A deal is signed between the British government and the banks that promises funding to shore up the financial institutions' ailing finances. In total £500 billion is provided to prevent a banking collapse in the middle of a global financial crisis. The deal means that some banks are effectively nationalised. The issue also sees bankers' image tarnished. A second bailout is announced only a few months later.

(Wednesday 8 October 2008)

5.30 a.m.

Krakatoa experiences a massive explosion. It is the first in a series of four blasts on a day that destroys the Indonesian volcano itself. The noise of the explosions can be heard over 3,000 miles away. Tsunamis are started by the volcanic activity and, along with the lava flows and ash clouds, cause a final death toll estimated to reach almost 40,000, although some believe it is much higher. The effect of the ash cloud on the upper atmosphere is believed to have inspired the red sky in Edvard Munch's painting 'The Scream'.

(Monday 27 August 1883)

5.30 a.m.

Mexican troops start to enter the Alamo, a fortress built by the Spanish in the eighteenth century. Those fighting for Texas have held out against a much larger Mexican force for almost two weeks. The leader of the Texas Army, William Travis, has sent urgent calls for reinforcements, ending one of them: 'Victory or Death.' Unfortunately for almost all of the few hundred inside, it is death. Among those who die are Davy Crockett and Jim Bowie, who give their names to items of clothing and equipment respectively. The heroic nature of the Texans' demise acts as inspiration for others, and a few months later Texas is declared an independent republic.

(Sunday 6 March 1836)

5.50 a.m.

The FBI enters the compound of the Branch Davidians at Waco in Texas. The cult, led by David Koresh, withstood a similar attempt a few months previously. This assault ends in disaster as over seventy members of the sect die, some through gunfire, others from fire or collapsing buildings.

(Monday 19 April 1993)

5.52 a.m.

The first successful human heart transplant operation is completed. A thirty-strong team, led by South African heart surgeon Christiaan Barnard, performed the 5-hour operation. Louis Washkansky, a 55-year-old man suffering from terminal heart disease, has received the heart of a woman seriously injured in a road accident. Rather than waiting until her heart had stopped, Barnard injected potassium into it before removing it. His achievement makes him world-renowned. The recipient dies from pneumonia eighteen days after the operation.

(Sunday 3 December 1967)

6.00 A.M. TO 6.59 A.M.

6.00 a.m.

After crossing the Pacific Ocean, a journey that has taken almost 100 days, a member of Ferdinand Magellan's crew spots land. It is the Marianas Islands, which they have reached after an epic journey that has seen them run out of food and resort to eating leather. They are the first Westerners to cross the Pacific from the east. Magellan names the ocean 'Pacific' as it is so calm when they first encounter it. The Portuguese had set off from Seville in September 1519 to seek a route to the Spice Islands in South East Asia. Although he is killed by islanders in the Philippines, the remaining few members of his crew reach Spain in 1522 and are the first to circumnavigate the globe.

(Wednesday 6 March 1521)

6.00 a.m.

Sir Walter Raleigh sails from Cork for Guiana. He had been imprisoned in the Tower of London for thirteen years and was released to lead this expedition. He doesn't find gold, and his men, including his son Wat, attack the Spaniards they encounter. This infuriates the Spanish ambassador in England, who demands Raleigh's head. On asking to see the axe to be used for his execution, Raleigh says: 'This is a sharp medicine but is a sound cure for all diseases.' Raleigh had been a favourite of Queen Elizabeth I; the story of him laying his cloak down for her to step on may be true. Raleigh was responsible for popularising tobacco smoking in Britain and may have introduced the potato to Ireland.

(Saturday 19 August 1617)

6.00 a.m.

The Black Hole of Calcutta is opened. British, Dutch and Indian prisoners have been kept overnight in a room big enough only for six people. As many as 123 prisoners have died in the cramped cell, although the total number is disputed. The nawab in charge, Siraj-ud-Daulah, is later deposed by Robert Clive.

(Monday 21 June 1756)

6.00 a.m.

Giacomo Casanova fears his escape attempt may be foundering. Trapped in a room following a rooftop escape, he puts on his best clothes and opens a window. He is spotted, and minutes later a doorkeeper unlocks the room and Casanova and his fellow escapee Father Balbi are free. Casanova has been imprisoned in the Doge's Palace in Venice for 'grave faults committed … primarily in public outrages against the holy religion'. He embarks on a grand tour of Europe and becomes involved in numerous schemes to earn money. His name becomes synonymous with a flamboyant and promiscuous lifestyle.

(Monday 1 November 1756)

6.00 a.m.

Europeans see Eastern Australia for the first time. British navigator Captain Cook had been searching for the possible continent *Terra Australis Incognita* – the unknown southern land. Cook wrote that the country 'had a very agreeable and promising aspect'. He later makes a landing at a place he initially calls Stingray Bay but then changes the name to Botany Bay. It later becomes a destination for the first white settlers, many of whom are transported convicts.

(Friday 20 April 1770)

6.00 a.m.

The night watchman at Westminster Abbey discovers that the Stone of Destiny is missing. The ancient symbol of Scottish coronations has resided in England since being stolen by Edward I in 1296. Scottish nationalists have taken the stone northwards in an act called a 'coarse and vulgar crime' by *The Times* newspaper. The stone is later returned to London but is repatriated to Scotland under the Conservative government in 1996. There is some speculation that this is not the original, as the caretakers had ample time to hide the actual stone before Edward I arrived at Scone.

(Monday 25 December 1950)

6.00 a.m.

Westminster Abbey opens to receive the first guests for the day's historic event. Elizabeth II is to be crowned in a coronation ceremony broadcast live on television for the first time. An estimated 3 million throng the streets of London to catch a glimpse of the procession. Elizabeth succeeded King George VI whose last public appearance was to say farewell as Elizabeth and her husband Prince Philip left for an African tour. Although the king had a crippling stammer that inhibited public appearances and hadn't been brought up to rule as monarch, he earned respect by remaining in London throughout the Blitz.

(Tuesday 2 June 1953)

6.00 a.m.: Westminster Abbey opens. (Lacihobo, Creative Commons)

6.00 a.m.

Guyanese troops arrive at Jonestown to find over 900 men, women and children lying dead. The compound is the home of the People's Temple Agricultural Project, a religious cult led by American Jim Jones. Jones had urged his followers to kill themselves by drinking a fruit drink mixed with cyanide. Those that didn't volunteer were forced to drink at gunpoint. Infants died after having the poison squirted into their mouths with syringes. Jones had said: 'Death is a million times preferable to 10 more days of this life.'

(Sunday 19 November 1978)

6.07 a.m.

Myra Hindley's brother-in-law David Smith telephones Manchester Police. He has witnessed Hindley's boyfriend Ian Brady kill a 17-year-old called Edward Evans with an axe. Police arrest Brady, who at trial is found guilty of the murder of Evans and two other children. Hindley is also found guilty of two murders. The crimes are known as the Moors Murders as Hindley and Brady bury four of their five known victims on Saddleworth Moor. The two are despised for the horrific murders when it is revealed that they tape-recorded the torture and killing of 10-year-old Lesley Anne Downey. One victim, Keith Bennett, is never found, and the search for his body continues on the moorland.

(Thursday 7 October 1965)

6.07 a.m.

Journalist Andrew Gilligan broadcasts a story on BBC Radio 4's *Today* programme. He reports that the government have included an erroneous claim in the dossier outlining the threat posed by Saddam Hussein's 'weapons of mass destruction'. The story leads to government attacks on the BBC and the unveiling of Gilligan's source. Weapons inspector Dr David Kelly is subjected to intense press attention and aggressive questioning at a Commons committee hearing. Dr Kelly's body is found in woods a few days later. The formal inquiry into Kelly's death states that it was caused by suicide, although doubts are aired by politicians and medical professionals.

(Thursday 29 May 2003)

6.10 a.m.

Serial killer Harold Shipman is found in his cell in Wakefield Prison. The ex-doctor has hanged himself. He was convicted of fifteen murders but it is thought he may have killed as many as 215 people.

(Tuesday 13 January 2004)

6.10 a.m.

Hurricane Katrina makes landfall over Louisiana. Winds are measured at 125mph. A storm surge breaches many New Orleans levees, flooding 80 per cent of the city. The aftermath sees local and national authorities heavily criticised for not reacting quickly enough or in a coordinated manner. Katrina causes $80 billion worth of damage and over 1,800 people are killed.

(Monday 29 August 2005)

6.40 a.m.

The first current of electricity passes through William Kemmler, the first convicted criminal to be sentenced to death on the newly invented electric chair. Famed American inventor Thomas Edison is using the issue to establish the adoption of his preferred DC form of electricity rather than the AC advocated by his rival George Westinghouse. Edison hopes to discredit AC by showing it to be unsafe as it is capable of killing a human. Dogs, cats, cows, horses and even an orang-utan have been killed through AC demonstrations. Kemmler's electrocution does not go smoothly and he is subjected to an 8-minute ordeal before succumbing. One of the witnesses says afterwards: 'I would rather see 10 hangings than one such execution as this.' The 'Battle of the Currents' is won by Westinghouse.

(Wednesday 6 August 1890)

7.00 A.M. TO 7.59 A.M.

7.00 a.m.

Captain Cook leaves his ship, HMS *Resolution*, to retrieve a boat taken by natives on Hawaii. The action leads to Cook being killed along with four marines. Parts of Cook's remains are eventually handed back and buried at sea. He is remembered as one of the great explorers, especially for his achievements in the exploration of the Pacific Ocean in three voyages, including the first European visits to Hawaii and Easter Island, and the first crossing of the Antarctic Circle.

(Sunday 14 February 1779)

7.00 a.m.

The last inhabitants leave St Kilda. The group of islands – 40 miles out in the Atlantic from the Outer Hebrides – have been inhabited for two millennia. The St Kildans' way of life has changed little over the centuries but emigration and illness have made life there unsustainable.

(Friday 29 August 1930)

7.00 a.m.

The ship *Empire Windrush* arrives at London's Tilbury Docks from the Caribbean. It carries over 1,000 passengers, around half of whom are West Indian immigrants looking for work. There is some concern over this immigration, reflected in a letter sent to the Labour Prime Minister Clement Attlee by some of his MPs, who write: 'An influx of coloured people domiciled here is likely to impair the harmony, strength and cohesion of our public and social life and to cause discord and unhappiness among all concerned.' The *Empire Windrush*'s arrival is seen as a landmark symbol of a changing Britain.

(Tuesday 22 June 1948)

7.00 a.m.

NASA's space shuttle lifts off for the first time. The commander of *Columbia* is experienced astronaut John Young, flying with co-pilot Bob Crippen who is journeying into space for the first time. Young's heart rate at takeoff is 90 beats per minute. Crippen's is almost 50 per cent higher.

(Sunday 12 April 1981)

7.12 a.m.

Joseph Kittinger stands 102,800ft above the Earth. It has taken him an hour and half to reach this height in a balloon. Underneath his feet a sign reads: 'This is the highest step in the world'. Below him is 99 per cent of the Earth's atmosphere. Kittinger is taking part in tests on high-altitude parachute systems. He drops so quickly that he becomes the first person to go faster than the speed of sound without any propulsive means. Kittinger suffers a painful injury when his glove loses pressure and his hand swells up to twice its normal size. He later serves in Vietnam as a fighter pilot and is shot down, escaping by parachute.

(Tuesday 16 August 1960)

7.15 a.m.

Frenchman Philippe Petit begins a tightrope walk, 1,300ft above the streets of New York. He spends three quarters of an hour traversing between the two towers of the World Trade Center, at times sitting and lying down. He is arrested but no charges are brought.

(Wednesday 7 August 1974)

7.17 a.m.

Siberia experiences a huge explosion. Eighty square miles of forest near the Tunguska River are flattened by a blast equivalent to almost 200 Hiroshima bombs. The cause is an asteroid, over 100ft across and travelling at over 33,000mph, which explodes above the ground. Eye witnesses in Siberia report seeing a 'flying star' seconds before the explosion. The asteroid has an unusual effect on the atmosphere, with people in Britain seeing beautiful sunsets as late as 2.30 a.m. the next day.

(Tuesday 30 June 1908)

7.17 a.m.: Meteor hits the Tunguska area in Siberia. (Unknown)

7.18 a.m.

Buckingham Palace calls the police to inform them of an intruder in the queen's bedroom. The intruder is Michael Fagan, who has scaled the palace walls before climbing up a drainpipe to gain access to the palace's first floor. Fagan speaks to the queen for a period before being apprehended by a palace footman who has been out exercising the dogs. Fagan threatens to slash his own wrists in the queen's presence. His intrusion causes a political scandal over lapses in security. Fagan claims he did it because a voice in his head told him to. He had also drunk ten whiskies.

(Friday 9 July 1982)

7.20 a.m.

Brian Keenan leaves his villa to walk to work at Beirut University. He has just left the garden when a Mercedes pulls up. Four men get out and the Irishman is pushed into the back of the car. His incarceration by Islamic militiamen has begun, and it will be over four years until he is released.

Once free, he campaigns for the release of the other hostages, including his cellmate John McCarthy. Almost 100 Western hostages are taken between 1982 and 1992.

(Friday 11 April 1986)

7.28 a.m.

Torpedoes explode on the Russian nuclear-powered submarine *Kursk*. It sinks and 188 sailors are lost amid criticism that the Russian military take too long to seek international assistance. Twenty-three sailors are able to seek refuge in a rear part of the submarine, where they sit in total darkness until succumbing. One of the men writes a note by the light of his luminous watch. Captain Lieutenant Dmitri Kolesnikov ends: 'Let's hope that at least someone will read this. Regards to everybody. No need to despair. Kolesnikov.'

(Saturday 12 August 2000)

7.30 a.m.

Whistles blow along the line to signal troops to go 'over the top'. It is the first day of the Battle of the Somme. The preceding artillery bombardment hasn't been fully effective and German troops are able to inflict heavy casualties. Almost 60,000 British soldiers are injured or killed. British General Haig realises the campaign will be one of attrition rather than one of dramatic victories. Over 1 million troops from both sides will become casualties by the battle's end in November.

(Saturday 1 July 1916)

7.30 a.m.

Roberto Calvi is found hanging under London's Blackfriars Bridge. His pockets are filled with bricks and bank notes. Calvi, who has been missing for over a week, is the chairman of a bank with links to the Vatican and the mafia. It is claimed the manner of his death symbolises his association with an Italian Masonic lodge. His death is the subject of much speculation, with the original verdict of suicide being changed to that of open. Twenty years after his death a forensic report states he was murdered. Five people are charged with his murder but all are acquitted in an Italian court.

(Friday 18 June 1982)

7.40 a.m.

The SS *Politician* runs aground. The cargo boat is heading for America and Jamaica when it comes to grief off the Isle of Eriskay. The local population discover that the cargo is over 260,000 bottles of whisky and make efforts to salvage as much as they can. They manage to rescue 24,000 bottles. Some of the islanders are jailed following investigations by Customs and Excise. The wreck of the boat is blown up which provokes one of the locals to say: 'Dynamiting whisky? You wouldn't think there'd be men in the world so crazy as that.' The event is turned into a book and film called *Whisky Galore*.

(Wednesday 5 February 1941)

7.43 a.m.

Lowry Dairsley and Matt Rigby's third child is born. Harrison shares the same numeric time of birth as his two sisters, Ella and Evie, with Evie born at 7.43 in the evening. The odds of three children from the same family being born at the same time is over half a million to one. The father marks the events with a tattoo: 'Seven Forty Three'.

(Thursday 20 January 2011)

7.45 a.m.

The Six Day War begins as Israel launches surprise air strikes against Egypt. Fearing an invasion by Egypt, Syria and Jordan, the Jewish state has instigated a pre-emptive strike. Israeli forces take over the Sinai Desert, the West Bank, the Gaza Strip, the Golan Heights and all of Jerusalem. While it is an overwhelming victory, it leads to future issues with the occupied areas.

(Monday 5 June 1967)

7.52 a.m.

The evacuation of Saigon ends as the final Americans and Vietnamese are airlifted by helicopter from the compound of the American embassy. Hundreds of Vietnamese rush into the embassy grounds to await further flights but there is no escape. The communist North Vietnamese Army sweep into the city and the Vietnam War is over. Around 5 million Vietnamese died in the conflict, which had its origins in the 1940s but saw an escalation with American involvement in the 1960s. A large peace movement in the United States had opposed the war.

(Wednesday 30 April 1975)

7.59 a.m.

An earthquake occurs under the Indian Ocean, off the coast of Indonesia. The quake lasts for 10 minutes. The resulting tsunamis are the worst ever recorded, killing almost a quarter of a million people, with most of the dead in Indonesia. In places the wave height reaches 30m and the tsunami reaches as far as Antarctica, where tides rise by a metre. Humanitarian aid is rushed to the affected areas and prevents a medical emergency that would have caused even more deaths. The earthquake quickens the earth's rotation and also moves the north pole of the Earth by several centimetres.

(Sunday 26 December 2004)

8.00 A.M. TO 8.59 A.M.

8.00 a.m.

Joan of Arc is burned at the stake for heresy. The Maid of Orleans inspired France in the Hundred Years War against England with a famous victory at the Siege of Orleans. The following year she was captured and sold to the English, who put her on trial. Before her execution she asked for a cross to be held before her eyes, to which she prayed throughout. She was canonised as a saint in 1920.

(Wednesday 30 May 1431)

8.00 a.m.

Captain Bligh and eighteen of his men head away from HMS *Bounty* in a 23ft-long launch. A munity, under Fletcher Christian, has forced Bligh and his men off the ship. Their open boat begins an epic journey that covers 3,618 miles. Bligh's navigational achievement is all the more remarkable for being completed without the use of any charts.

(Tuesday 28 April 1789)

8.00 a.m.

Britain's era of capital punishment comes to an end with the hanging of two men. Peter Allen and Gwynne Evans are executed for the murder of John West. One is hanged in Manchester, the other in Liverpool. The last woman to be hanged was Ruth Ellis, who was executed in 1955.

(Thursday 13 August 1964)

8.05 a.m.

Bodysnatcher William Burke ascends the scaffold. With his partner William Hare, Burke has murdered at least fifteen people for the purposes of dissection at Edinburgh's College of Surgeons. Hare escaped punishment after turning king's evidence. There is much public interest in the case and notices are put up in Edinburgh's Grassmarket advertising 'windows to let' for the execution, with some viewing points going for a guinea. Over 20,000 turn up to see the hanging. Burke's body is taken for dissection at the university, where crowds are able to view his corpse.

(Wednesday 28 January 1829)

8.10 a.m.

Bombs fall on the USS *Arizona* at the Hawaiian port of Pearl Harbor. The majority of the crew are killed when the battleship rapidly sinks. Flying from aircraft carriers, Japanese aircraft cause widespread damage to the US Pacific Fleet and kill over 2,400 military personnel and civilians. The *Arizona* is the most notable target hit in the surprise raid. America declares war on Japan the next day and on Germany four days later.

(Sunday 7 December 1941)

8.15 a.m.

The first atomic bomb to be used in warfare is dropped. American B-29 bomber *Enola Gay* releases the weapon above the Japanese city of Hiroshima. The bomb, nicknamed 'Little Boy', explodes with a force of 15,000 tons of TNT. The flash imprints shadows onto the ground. Tens of thousands are killed in an instant and thousands more die in the following years from the effects of radiation. Although the death toll from the bomb is high, more have been killed in Japan by American conventional bombing with weapons such as incendiaries, which cause firestorms.

(Sunday 6 August 1945)

8.30 a.m.

A British officer is approached by four unarmed Germans on the Western Front. Captain Edward Hulse goes out to meet them and they converse for half an hour. The captain goes back to his headquarters to report. When he returns he sees his trenches empty. All his men are in no-man's-land, speaking and exchanging gifts with their German counterparts. The two enemies start singing songs to each other until they all combine to sing Robert Burns' 'Auld Lang Syne'. The events are just one example

8.15 a.m.: Atomic bomb is dropped on Hiroshima. (National Archives)

of the unofficial truces that sprung up along the line during the first Christmas of the First World War. They are seen as poignant examples of a common humanity between warring forces. Hulse is killed in 1915.

(Friday 25 December 1914)

8.32 a.m.

Mount St Helens erupts in Skamania County, Washington. The volcano has been triggered by an earthquake. Debris is blasted into the air at speeds of up to 670mph. The ash cloud causes the sun to be obscured and streetlights are automatically triggered. On the ground, an avalanche of rock debris flows at over 150mph. There is major devastation to the mountain, which loses over 1,300ft in height. Fifty-seven people are killed as a result of the eruption.

(Sunday 18 May 1980)

8.40 a.m.

The first non-stop transatlantic flight is completed successfully. Captain John Alcock and Lieutenant Arthur Brown have crossed the Atlantic in their Vickers Vimy twin-engined biplane, taking 16 hours to cover the 1,900 miles. The perilous flight, from Newfoundland to Clifden in western Ireland, has seen them fly as low as 20ft and combat heavy fog and freezing conditions. At times Brown climbed out of the cockpit to clear frozen ice from the engines. Alcock says: 'We have had a terrible voyage. The wonder is we are here at all.' They are both knighted for their achievement. Alcock is killed in an aircraft accident later that year but Brown never flies again.

(Sunday 15 June 1919)

8.43 a.m.

Amelia Earhart makes her last known radio transmission. The pioneer aviator is attempting a round-the-world flight with navigator Fred Noonan. They are heading for Howland Island from Papua New Guinea, a distance of over 2,500 miles. They and their Lockheed Electra aircraft are never found.

(Friday 2 July 1937)

8.45 a.m.

US President John F. Kennedy is briefed on the presence of Soviet nuclear missiles in Cuba. Photographs taken by a U-2 reconnaissance aircraft show SS-4 type missiles being set up. The missiles have a range that can reach almost all major US cities. Kennedy resolves to have the threat removed and the Cuban Missile Crisis threatens the world with nuclear devastation. The tense standoff is resolved thirteen days later when Russian leader Nikita Khrushchev agrees to have the missiles removed, on the condition that the USA promises not to invade Cuba. The Americans also agree to remove their own nuclear missiles from Turkey, a part of the deal that is kept secret for years.

(Tuesday 16 October 1962)

8.46 a.m.

American Airlines Flight 11 flies into the World Trade Center's North Tower. Minutes before, one of the cabin crew telephoned her airline's office and told them: 'Something is wrong. We are in a rapid descent.' Before the transmission ends, she is heard to say: 'Oh my god we are way too low.' Three other airliners have been hijacked. One flies into the South Tower, another hits the Pentagon in Washington and the last crashes in a field in Pennsylvania following an attempt by passengers and flight crew to retake control of the plane. Both towers collapse and almost 3,000 die. The 9/11 attacks lead to US military intervention in Afghanistan and Iraq.

(Tuesday 11 September 2001)

8.50 a.m.

Donald Campbell's boat *Bluebird* breaks up on Coniston Water while on a water speed record attempt. The jet-powered craft is travelling at more than 300mph when it lifts up then somersaults before hitting the water. Campbell is killed instantly.

(Wednesday 4 January 1967)

8.50 a.m.

Screens at the North American Aerospace Defence Command show an incoming missile raid. The defence system is designed to detect Russian intercontinental nuclear weapons being fired at Canada and the United States. Before America launches a retaliatory strike, checks are made with the detection systems. There is no raid. A technician had been running test tapes showing an attack that had gone through to the live system, giving a false alert.

(Friday 9 November 1979)

8.50 a.m.

Bombs go off on three London Underground trains. An hour later, another explodes on a London bus. Fifty-six people are killed and over 700 are injured in what become known as the 7/7 bombings. The devices, carried in rucksacks, have been set off by four male Muslim extremists. The day before, Londoners had celebrated the announcement that the city would be hosting the 2012 Olympic Games.

(Thursday 7 July 2005)

8.53 a.m.

A U-2 spy plane, operated by the CIA, is hit by a missile over Russia. Pilot Francis Gary Powers is forced to parachute from his stricken aircraft. The Americans claim it is a weather flight but Powers isn't able to destroy the photographic equipment on board and a diplomatic incident arises. He is sentenced to ten years imprisonment for spying but is released from a Soviet jail, two years later, and returns to the West through a spy-exchange programme.

(Sunday 1 May 1960)

8.56 a.m.

A rocket is fired into space carrying the ashes of two astronauts, one fictional and one real. The remains are those of actor James Doohan who played Scotty on the USS *Enterprise* in the *Star Trek* TV show, and astronaut Gordon Cooper who flew into space on the *Mercury-Atlas 9* and *Gemini V* missions.

(Saturday 28 April 2007)

9.00 A.M. TO 9.59 A.M.

9.00 a.m.

William, Duke of Normandy, orders his troops forward. They face the army of King Harold, who has taken up a position outside Hastings in the south of England. During the battle Harold is killed, possibly by an arrow in the eye, and William 'the Conqueror' becomes the first Norman King of England. The Normans' influence on English society is widespread and they carry out a survey of the country, collated in the Domesday Book. William's invasion is depicted in a large embroidery kept in Bayeux, Normandy.

(Saturday 14 October 1066)

9.00 a.m.

Saladin begins his attack on King Richard I's troops, outside the town of Arsuf. The Saracens' assault is held off while Richard delays his response. At a critical point he sends his cavalry in, which produces a notable victory. King Richard, known as the Lionheart, is making his way to recapture Jerusalem as part of the Third Crusade. Saladin is able to retain Jerusalem despite his emphatic defeat. Richard is noted for his military prowess, but for a national heroic icon, he only spends six months of his ten-year reign in England. He dies in Normandy while at war with the French King Philip II, his previous ally in the crusade.

(Saturday 7 September 1191)

9.00 a.m.

Anne Boleyn is executed at the Tower of London, having been found guilty of trumped-up charges of adultery and incest. She was Henry VIII's second wife and was unable to produce a male heir. Henry's desire for Anne had helped bring about the Reformation in England, as the Catholic

Church would not grant him a divorce from his first wife, Catherine of Aragon. Henry marries six times and has another wife, Catherine Howard, executed. The evening before her beheading, Anne had joked that she might be nicknamed 'Queen Lackhead'. She does produce an heir: her daughter Elizabeth becomes Queen in 1558 and reigns for forty-four years.

(Friday 19 May 1536)

9.00 a.m.

Merchant Taylor's Hall in London is crammed with investors keen to hear news of the South Sea Company from its directors. The company, which has taken on the national debt, has seen the value of its shares rise from £128 each in January to over £1,000 in August. However, the price has fallen dramatically as the investment 'bubble' starts to burst. The gathered crowd are not reassured by the directors, who have sold their own holdings for healthy profits. Many investors lose money. One of them is Sir Isaac Newton, who had sold his shares at a profit, but then bought more at a high price. He loses £20,000. He writes: 'I can calculate the motions of the heavenly bodies, but not the madness of people.'

(Sunday 8 September 1720)

9.00 a.m.

Florence Nightingale arrives at Constantinople in Turkey. She has gone to administer a military hospital in Scutari for troops fighting in the Crimean War. She gains a reputation for being 'the lady with the lamp' as she goes on her nightly rounds. After two years she returns to Britain to great acclaim, which she shuns. Florence Nightingale is remembered for her Crimean work but her major legacy is the laying down of many of the foundations of modern nursing.

(Saturday 4 November 1854)

9.00 a.m.

Derek Bentley is hanged. He has been sentenced to death for his part in the shooting of a policeman during a robbery. Although 19 years old, Bentley has the mental age of someone aged 11 or 12. In the trial it is heard that Bentley had said to his fellow accused, Christopher Craig,

9.00 a.m.: Florence Nightingale arrives in Constantinople. (Unknown)

who had a gun, to 'Let him have it, Chris'. Whether he meant Craig to hand the gun over or start firing isn't known. Bentley is sentenced to death while the younger Craig is given life imprisonment. The day before his execution, Bentley is visited by his parents and his sister. On their departure he says to them: 'Cheerio, dad. Cheerio, mum. Cheerio, Iris. I'll see you tomorrow.' The execution of a teenager adds to the weight of argument for those opposed to Britain's death penalty.

(Wednesday 28 January 1953)

9.00 a.m.

The order is issued for the population of Phnom Penh to leave the city. The Khmer Rouge under Pol Pot have taken over after five years of civil war. The new government initiates severe measures such as mass urban evacuations and forced labour. Attacks are made on the 'elite' – government or professional workers who are seen as less worthy than the agrarian peasants. It is later estimated that between 1.7 and 2.5 million Cambodians die from starvation, disease or violence. Only a tenth of the country's doctors remain alive. Pol Pot is ousted after an invasion by Vietnam in 1979.

(Thursday 17 April 1975)

9.00 a.m.

Runners start to move off in the first London Marathon. It takes 6 minutes for all 6,500 entrants to cross the start line. The first male runners to finish hold hands as they cross the line in 2 hours 11 minutes. Disc jockey and television presenter Jimmy Saville takes part in the race, raising £50,000 for charity.

(Sunday 29 March 1981)

9.00 a.m.

Rock Hudson dies of complications caused by AIDS. The Hollywood actor had announced that he had the condition when seeking treatment in Paris a few months before. He had kept his homosexuality secret from the public throughout his acting career. Hudson's revelations shocked many who had only known him as the handsome screen star of movies such as *Pillow Talk* and *Giant*. It helps to change perceptions of AIDS, a disease that has killed 30 million people by 2011.

(Wednesday 2 October 1985)

9.00 a.m.

The Millennium Bridge in London opens for the second time. It had been closed three days after opening in 2000 after it developed a wobble. £5 million was spent on fixing the lateral vibrations on the Norman Foster-designed construction.

(Friday 22 February 2002)

9.00 a.m.

The tallest bridge in the world opens to traffic. Cars travelling on the Millau Viaduct are 890ft off the ground. The span curves 1.5 miles over the Tarn River Valley in southern France. It instantly becomes an icon of

Anglo-French design and construction, designed by Sir Norman Foster and built by French company Eiffage, who had previously built the Eiffel Tower and the Statue of Liberty.

(Thursday 16 December 2004)

9.00 a.m.

Harry Patch dies, aged 111. He is the last surviving soldier to have fought in the First World War – the last of almost 6 million. He hadn't spoken about the war until eighty years after it had ended. Patch had been injured in 1917 at Ypres and was recuperating when the armistice was signed. He was fervently anti-war and keen to show the futility of conflict where millions could be killed over territorial dispute or in a 'family row' as he described the First World War. He said: 'War isn't worth one life.'

(Saturday 25 July 2009)

9.03 a.m.

The *Mary Rose* is seen above the River Solent for the first time in 437 years. The ship, which was built for King Henry VIII, was sunk in 1545 in an engagement with French ships. The king watched from the shore as his flagship tipped over and disappeared beneath the waves. Only around thirty members of the crew were saved from its complement of over 400. The salvage operation almost ends in disaster when part of the lifting structure breaks and threatens to crush part of the ship.

(Monday 11 October 1982)

9.04 a.m.

On a US warship, the Japanese foreign minister is first to sign the formal Instruments of Surrender. Twenty minutes later the formalities are complete and the Second World War is officially over. Estimates vary but at least 50 million people have died as a result of the conflict.

(Sunday 2 September 1945)

9.05 a.m.

The production line at the Volkswagen factory in Peubla, Mexico, is switched off as the manufacturing of a legendary motorcar ends. The last

Beetle of 21,529,464 is ceremonially rolled out of the plant. More Beetles have been produced than any other car, beating the Ford Model T by 6 million. The Beetle had been developed during the 1930s in Germany, where it had originally been designated the 'KdF-Wagen' (*Kraft durch Freude* – Strength Through Joy). It later became known as the Volkswagen, or 'people's car'.

(Wednesday 30 July 2003)

9.07 a.m.

Yuri Gagarin is on his way to becoming the first human in space as he launches from Baikonur in Kazakhstan in the *Vostok 1* spacecraft. The single orbit flight lasts 108 minutes. The world's first cosmonaut says while in space: 'The earth is blue. How wonderful. It is amazing.' On his return he is celebrated around the world. Gagarin never flies in space again and later dies in a mysterious aircraft accident.

(Wednesday 12 April 1961)

9.15 a.m.

Bonnie Parker and Clyde Barrow are ambushed. The notorious couple are wanted by the authorities for a series of murders, robberies and kidnappings across five states of America. Their whereabouts are tracked down and lawmen line a road in Louisiana waiting for their Ford car. Reports conflict as to whether a warning was given or whether the pair were fired on without notice. Both die in a hail of bullets and their car becomes a museum attraction.

(Wednesday 23 May 1934)

9.15 a.m.

A slag heap collapses in the Welsh mining village of Aberfan. The landslide moves thousands of tons of debris, which engulfs a junior school, a farm and some houses. Of the 144 people killed, 116 of them are children. The school's deputy head teacher was found dead later that night. A rescuer said: 'He was clutching five children in his arms as if he had been protecting them.' The National Coal Board is blamed for the disaster. A mass burial a week later sees 10,000 mourners attending.

(Friday 21 October 1966)

9.22 a.m.

In Saigon, a Buddhist monk sets himself on fire. Thích Quảng Đức is making a protest against the government's unequal treatment of Buddhists. The event is captured by a news photographer and the shocking images are seen all over the world. The act becomes a pivotal moment in the country's history, leading to the downfall of the Diệm government. Đức's body is cremated as part of his funeral and his still intact heart is kept as a religious relic.

(Tuesday 11 June 1963)

9.25 a.m.

Lorries carrying coke start to leave the Orgreave coking plant in South Yorkshire. Miners picketing to halt such deliveries push forward against police lines. The ensuing 'Battle of Orgreave' sees over 100 miners and policemen injured, including National Union of Miners' leader Arthur Scargill. He describes it as 'a scene reminiscent of a battle in England's 17th century civil war.' Over ninety picketers are arrested but none are convicted. Orgreave is the violent focal point of a bitter dispute over the future of the coal mining industry in Britain. After a year, the miners return to work. The mining industry enters a period of decline and by 2005 over 150 mines out of the 170 open at the start of the strike are closed.

(Monday 18 June 1984)

9.29 a.m.

A 70-year-old man is killed in a road accident in the Finnish town of Raahe. Two and a quarter hours later, another elderly man is killed. The two men are twin brothers. Both are hit by trucks while out riding their bikes and both accidents happen on the same road.

(Tuesday 5 March 2002)

9.40 a.m.

An American B-25 Mitchell bomber hits the Empire State Building. The pilot has found himself among New York's skyscrapers while flying in thick fog. He tries to pull away but his aircraft hits what is then the world's tallest building between the 78th and 79th floors. Lift cables are severed and the cars plummet to the ground. One of the women inside, Betty

Lou Oliver, was injured in the initial impact and is being sent down to receive medical aid. She survives but fourteen others die in the incident.

(Saturday 28 July 1945)

9.45 a.m.

The last Union Army survivor of the American Civil War dies, aged 106. Albert Woolson served as a bugler-drummer in the Union Army. Woolson had voted for Lincoln in 1864's presidential elections. Although not a combatant in the war, he did get to fire a cannon with the artillery unit he was assigned. He said: 'It scared me half to death.' He was the last living soldier of the 2,200,000 who served with the Union forces.

(Thursday 2 August 1956)

9.45 a.m.

The foreperson reads out the verdict of the State of California versus Orenthal James Simpson. The ex-American football star has been charged with murdering his wife Nicole Brown Simpson and her friend Ron Goldman. Half of America's population watch as the highly publicised trial comes to an end and O.J. Simpson is acquitted. He is jailed for armed robbery and kidnapping in 2008.

(Tuesday 3 October 1995)

10.00 A.M. TO 10.59 A.M.

10.00 a.m.

A fleet of over 450 vessels enters the Strait of Dover. Travelling on the ship *Brill* is the Dutch ruler, Prince William. He lands at Torbay with a force of 21,000 troops, mainly Dutch. William becomes King William III in 1689, with his wife Anne (James' daughter) becoming queen. Their Protestant monarchy replaces that of the Catholic James VII & II who has fled the country. Although described as a 'Glorious Revolution' there is subsequent violence in Ireland and Scotland. It also sees the start of a period of Jacobitism, with Catholic supporters hoping to restore a Stuart monarch.

(Saturday 3 November 1688)

10.00 a.m.

David Livingstone sails for the African mainland for the last time. He is leaving Zanzibar to find the source of the River Nile. Livingstone had spent a large part of his life exploring Africa and was the first Westerner to cross the whole continent. On his last expedition he finds himself stranded and stricken with illness and reliant on the slave traders he abhors. An expedition led by Welshman John Rowlands – who had changed his name to Henry Stanley after emigrating to America – reaches the Scotsman in 1871. Stanley's first words are reportedly: 'Doctor Livingstone, I presume'. Livingstone doggedly remains in Africa but dies in 1873. His heart is buried before friends carry his body to the coast from where it is returned to Britain.

(Monday 19 March 1866)

10.00 a.m.

Yale lecturer Hiram Bingham leaves his camp in the Andean mountains. After a strenuous climb, a local guide leads him to the hilltop ruins of

Machu Picchu. He is not the first westerner to see the former Inca site but he is the first who is able to bring it to widespread attention. The site becomes a popular visitor attraction, which, despite its isolated location, receives 400,000 visitors a year.

(Monday 24 July 1911)

10.00 a.m.

British Army officer T.E. Lawrence enters the Red Sea port of Aqaba. Lawrence's daring mission has seen him journey 600 miles across inhospitable desert terrain. Lawrence of Arabia's alliance with the Arabs in revolt against the Turks gains him a legendary reputation, which he is both keen to promote and shy away from. After the war he seeks anonymity by joining the RAF as a non-commissioned serviceman. Lawrence dies in 1935 following a motorcycle accident.

(Friday 6 July 1917)

10.00 a.m.

Five men get out of a car in Chicago's Clark Street. Armed with machine guns, they go inside a garage. The gangsters line seven men up against a wall and gun them down in cold blood in one of organised crime's most notorious events: the St Valentine's Day Massacre. Mobster Al Capone is rumoured to be behind the murders, but no one is ever charged. Capone is eventually jailed for tax evasion.

(Thursday 14 February 1929)

10.00 a.m.

Edward VIII signs the Instrument of Abdication. After less than a year as monarch, the uncrowned king steps down to pursue his love for Wallis Simpson, an American woman whose status as a divorcee is judged to be unsuitable for a king's wife. Edward is the first British monarch to give up the crown in over 500 years. That evening he tells the nation and the Commonwealth in a radio broadcast: 'I have found it impossible to carry the heavy burden of responsibility and to discharge my duties as King as I would wish to do without the help and support of the woman I love.' They marry in 1937 and remain together until Edward's death in 1972.

(Thursday 10 December 1936)

10.00 a.m.

In a cinema in Los Angeles the cast and crew are given a preview screening of the film they have just completed. Written and directed by George Lucas, the film is called *Star Wars*. It opens on general release a few days later. It is a huge success, and becomes one of the highest-grossing films of all time. It makes stars of Harrison Ford, Carrie Fisher and Mark Hamill, who plays the central character Luke Skywalker. Five more *Star Wars* films are made, although none have the impact or appeal of the first.

(Saturday 21 May 1977)

10.00 a.m.

Britain's first civil partnership ceremony gets underway. Protestors and supporters stand outside Belfast's City Hall as Shannon Sickles and Grainne Close go through the ceremony to achieve the same legal rights as heterosexual couples.

(Monday 19 December 2005)

10.06 a.m.

Jean Charles de Menezes has just boarded the London Underground train at Stockwell station when officers from the Metropolitan Police open fire. He is hit in the head by seven bullets and dies instantly. An inquest finds that he is killed as a result of mistaken identity, the security forces believing him to be a terrorist suspect. The shooting takes place during a period of heightened alert following the 7/7 bombings in London two weeks previously and a failed Underground bombing the day before.

(Friday 22 July 2005)

10.30 a.m.

Soldiers from the Gloucestershire Regiment make their escape bid from positions on Hill 235. Chinese forces have crossed the Imjin River to get to the South Korean capital of Seoul and have encircled the 'Glosters'. For four days British troops have stopped their advance, defending a key position against overwhelming odds. Casualties are heavy and only thirty-nine men make it back to meet up with friendly forces. The action has had its intended effect, allowing Seoul to be defended. The Korean War drags on for another two years before a peace agreement is signed.

(Wednesday 25 April 1951)

10.30 a.m.

The trial of Penguin Books begins at the Old Bailey in London. The publisher has been charged with offences under the Obscene Publications Act over D.H. Lawrence's book *Lady Chatterley's Lover.* The trial is won by Penguin, which immediately sees huge sales of the book. The much-publicised trial is viewed as being one part of the easing of the restrictive society of the 1950s and allowing the 'swinging sixties' to begin.

(Thursday 20 October 1960)

10.30 a.m.

Georgi Markov is admitted to hospital, suffering from a high temperature. The Bulgarian had felt a sharp pain in his right leg while walking on Waterloo Bridge the previous day. He looked around to see a man picking up an umbrella. Markov, a dissident who defected to the West in 1969, works for the BBC, making broadcasts to Bulgaria. He dies of ricin poisoning three days after the attack. Markov's post-mortem finds a metal ball, less than 2mm in diameter, in his leg, fired by a mechanism inside an umbrella.

(Friday 8 September 1978)

10.30 a.m.

Mhairi Isabel MacBeath is pronounced dead on arrival at Stirling's Royal Infirmary. She is the seventeenth and last victim of a massacre that has taken place in a primary school in the Scottish town of Dunblane. Class 1/13 were in the school's gymnasium when the gunman began firing. The class's teacher was shot dead while attempting to protect the children. It is one of Britain's worst civilian atrocities. The gunman avoids arrest by shooting himself.

(Wednesday 13 March 1996)

10.30 a.m.

Britain's coxless fours rowing team start off in the final of their event in the Sydney Olympics. On board is four-times gold-medal winner Steve Redgrave. With him is Matthew Pinsent, James Cracknell and Tim Foster. After a close race they edge out their Italian rivals' boat by less than half a second. Redgrave enters Olympic fame as the only athlete to win five gold medals in successive games. Pinsent wins his third gold, Cracknell his second and Foster his first.

(Saturday 23 September 2000)

10.32 a.m.

Aron Ralston takes the first step to free himself. He has been trapped in a narrow canyon 100ft below ground level in Utah's Canyonlands. After a fall his right arm had been caught under a large boulder. On the sixth day after becoming trapped, Ralston cuts his own arm off with a knife. Bleeding heavily and in shock, he makes his way out of the canyon and is able to reach help. He later cremates the severed arm and scatters the ashes in the canyon.

(Thursday 1 May 2003)

10.35 a.m.

Orville Wright makes the world's first successful powered flight. On the beach at Kitty Hawk in North Carolina, the aircraft designed by Orville and his brother Wilbur flies for around 12 seconds, travels 120ft and takes a giant leap forward. The brothers make three other flights that day until their historic craft is damaged by wind. It never flies again.

(Thursday 17 December 1903)

10.39 a.m.

The Earth shows its face. For the first time a full view of the Earth can be seen. *Apollo 17* astronauts heading for the moon take an image that becomes one of the most widely reproduced photographs in history. The sun is behind their spacecraft, and their trajectory affords them a memorable view. The image gains the title 'The Blue Marble'.

(Thursday 7 December 1972)

10.35 a.m.: Orville Wright takes to the air. (J.T. Daniels, USLSS)

10.40 a.m.

The world's first inter-city passenger railway opens. To mark the occasion, a special procession of locomotives carrying eminent figures such as the Duke of Wellington and Robert Peel, leaves Liverpool for Manchester. Huge crowds line the route, keen to see the famous passengers and this new method of transportation. The event is tainted with tragedy as one of the passengers is hit by George Stephenson's *Rocket* locomotive during a scheduled stop and dies after having his leg almost severed by the wheels.

(Wednesday 15 September 1830)

10.40 a.m.

Archduke Franz Ferdinand is shot. On a visit to the city of Sarajevo, the heir to the Austro-Hungarian Empire and his wife are killed by Gavrilo Princip, a Bosnian-Serb student. The incident sparks the beginning of the First World War after Austria-Hungary declares war on Serbia.

(Sunday 28 June 1914)

10.45 a.m.

Boxers Muhammad Ali and Joe Frazier begin their third bout together in a fight dubbed 'The Thrilla in Manilla'. Ali retains his world heavyweight championship title after fourteen bruising rounds. Frazier's manager refuses to let his boxer carry on, saying to him: 'No one will ever forget what you did here today.' The fight takes its toll on Ali who says it was 'the closest thing to dying that I know of.' Ali's boxing prowess, quick wittedness, brash self-publicising, and moral standpoint on refusing to be enlisted into the Vietnam War, make him one of the most famous sportsmen in the world.

(Wednesday 1 October 1975)

10.59 a.m.

Private Henry Gunther is shot. With the armistice due to end the war at 11.00 a.m., Gunther is part of a US Army unit advancing on a German machine-gun position near the French town of Metz. The Germans wave the troops back, unwilling to cause any more deaths so close to the imminent end of the fighting. Gunther charges with his bayonet and is shot and killed immediately. His divisional record states: 'Almost as he fell the gunfire died away and an appalling silence prevailed.' Gunther was of German immigrant descent. He is the last official casualty of the First World War.

(Monday 11 November 1918)

11.00 A.M. TO MIDDAY

11.00 a.m.

The First World War is officially over as the ceasefire comes into effect. The four-year Great War has resulted in 37 million casualties, with a total of 16 million civilians and soldiers killed. An estimated 11,000 soldiers are injured or killed on the final day.

(Monday 11 November 1918)

11.00 a.m.

Britain declares war on Germany. The British government had issued Adolf Hitler with an ultimatum over Germany's military actions against Poland, but when the Germans continue their offensive, Britain announces that it would fulfil its obligations towards Poland. France also declares war on Germany. A period known as the 'Phoney War' begins, as there is little initial military action.

(Sunday 3 September 1939)

11.00 a.m.

Britain's first motorway opens. Prime Minister Harold MacMillan performs the opening ceremony and then takes a drive along the 8¼-mile stretch of the Preston bypass. The Automobile Association announce that due to the speed and volume of traffic, their patrolmen won't always be able to make their traditional greeting of a salute to association members.

(Friday 5 December 1958)

11.00 a.m.

Australian TV personality and naturalist Steve Irwin is stung by a stingray. The Australian 'Crocodile Hunter' is filming a documentary in the Great

Barrier Reef when he is attacked. He dies shortly afterwards.

(Monday 4 September 2006)

11.02 a.m.

Three days after the first atomic bomb is dropped on Hiroshima, a second is dropped on Japan by America. The city of Nagasaki suffers tens of thousands of casualties. The previous day, the Soviet Union had declared war on Japan. Despite the Japanese Army's wish to carry on, Emperor Hirohito orders his country's surrender. He speaks to his nation in a radio broadcast, the first time the Japanese people hear his voice.

(Thursday 9 August 1945)

11.05 a.m.

John Profumo makes a statement to the House of Commons in which he states: 'There was no impropriety whatsoever in my acquaintanceship with Miss Keeler.' Profumo, the secretary of state for war, is embroiled in a scandal involving an affair between himself and the 19-year-old Christine Keeler, who had also been sleeping with a Russian naval attaché. Profumo is forced to resign ten weeks later. The scandal discredits the Conservative government of the time and Profumo, who never discusses the affair, leaves politics for charity work in London's East End.

(Friday 22 March 1963)

11.08 a.m.

The Tacoma Narrows bridge collapses. Due to strong winds, the road bridge was affected by a condition known as 'aeroelastic flutter'. A 16mm ciné film is made of *Galloping Gertie* – named because of its capacity for moving in wind – as it twists and turns. At times it tilts to a 45-degree angle, raising the road almost 30ft up on one side, before falling into Puget Sound. The bridge's destruction changes the way future suspension bridges are built.

(Thursday 7 November 1940)

11.10 a.m.

The Light Cavalry Brigade begin their charge at Balaclava. They make their way into the 'Valley of Death' galloping towards the Russian lines,

11.10 a.m.: Charge of the Light Brigade. (Library of Congress)

encountering savage artillery and rifle fire from each side. They suffer horrendous casualties, with almost half the force injured, killed or taken prisoner, and are forced to retreat after just 25 minutes. Their futile action is the result of a misunderstanding. Lord Cardigan's cavalrymen were not ordered to take on the full might of the Russian forces, but to secure abandoned Turkish guns that the Russians had captured. The Crimean War saw the Russian Empire fighting an alliance featuring Britain, France, the Turkish Ottoman Empire and Sardinia.

(Wednesday 25 October 1854)

11.17 a.m.

Donald Crowhurst writes the penultimate entry in his logbook. He writes: 'I have not need to prolong the game.' 'The game' is a deception. Crowhurst has entered a solo, non-stop, round-the-world sailing race. Very soon after setting out he discovers that his boat is not up to the task, but instead of returning home, he meanders aimlessly in the Atlantic. He then pretends that he has completed the circumnavigation and is just behind the leaders. Realising his fake logbooks won't stand up to scrutiny, Crowhurst gives up and descends into insanity. His catamaran is found a week later, with no sight of its sailor. The winner of the race, Robin Knox-Johnston, gives his £5,000 prize money to Crowhurst's family.

(Tuesday 1 July 1969)

11.20 a.m.

Edvard Munch's 'The Scream' is stolen. Armed thieves make a daylight raid on Oslo's Munch Museum and escape with the iconic depiction of despair and desolation in front of startled visitors. The painting is not recovered until two years later. Another version of 'The Scream' had also been stolen from the Norwegian National Museum in 1994. It was also recovered.

(Sunday 22 August 2004)

11.20 a.m.

Prince Charles and Lady Diana Spencer are married. Their lavish wedding is watched by an estimated TV audience of three quarters of a billion. A million people line the streets of London to see the procession, some of whom have camped out for two days. The couple delight the crowd with a much-anticipated kiss on Buckingham Palace's balcony. Lady Diana is 20 years old and Prince Charles is 32. They later divorce and Diana is killed in a road traffic accident in 1997.

(Wednesday 29 July 1981)

11.20 a.m.

The Archbishop of Canterbury proclaims Prince William and Kate Middleton man and wife. The couple, who met at St Andrews University, become the Duke and Duchess of Cambridge, Earl and Countess of Strathearn and Baron and Baroness Carrickfergus. William had proposed marriage to Kate with his mother's engagement ring.

(Friday 29 April 2011)

11.20 a.m.

Iraqi jets drop the first chemical weapons over the Iraqi Kurdish town of Halabja. The bombs contain mustard gas and several nerve agents. Over

5,000 are killed immediately with double that number injured. More succumb to the after effects of congenital abnormalities. The genocidal act was ordered by Saddam Hussein.

(Wednesday 16 March 1988)

11.21 a.m.

Two days after the death of President Kennedy, chief suspect Lee Harvey Oswald is shot by Jack Ruby, a nightclub owner, in Dallas, Texas. Oswald is being transferred from a police station to a jail when Ruby shoots at close range. The event is broadcast live on American television. Oswald had proclaimed his innocence of the murder of the president, saying: 'I'm just a patsy.' Ruby claims he killed him to ensure that Kennedy's widow Jacqueline didn't have to revisit Dallas for Oswald's trial.

(Sunday 24 November 1963)

11.21 a.m.

British worker Robert Fagg shakes hands with Frenchman Philippe Cozette as Britain becomes connected to the European continent for the first time in thousands of years. Tunnels being drilled from Britain and France meet under the English Channel in a technical achievement many thought impossible. Eurostar train services start within a few years.

(Saturday 1 December 1990)

11.30 a.m.

Marie Antoinette is beheaded by guillotine. The Queen of France had been sentenced to death for being 'guilty of having been accessory to and having cooperated in different manoeuvres against the Liberty of France'. She is an unpopular figure and her extravagance and remoteness from the majority of the population is seen as being partly to blame for the monarchy's decline. The French Revolution has torn through France and installed a republic after much bloodshed. Marie Antoinette is famous for saying 'let them eat cake' although the phrase was used 100 years before by another Marie – Marie-Therese, the wife of Louis XIV.

(Wednesday 16 October 1793)

11.30 a.m.

The world's highest mountain is climbed for the first time. The ascent to the 29,028ft summit of Mount Everest is achieved by New Zealander Edmund Hillary and Nepalese Tenzing Norgay. Who was first between the two men to step onto the top of the world is kept a secret for fifty years. Hillary says to the expedition members afterwards: 'We knocked the bastard off.'

(Friday 29 May 1953)

11.30 a.m.

In the Bay of Bengal, cargo ship MV *Mahajagmitra* reports hurricane-force winds. It sinks shortly afterwards. A tropical cyclone is moving north-east towards East Pakistan and eastern India. In places the Bhola Cyclone causes a storm surge over 30ft in height, which devastates the low-lying countryside of the Ganges Delta. Up to 500,000 lives are lost in one of the world's worst natural disasters. Political tensions rise afterwards as the Pakistan government is slow to react to the tragedy. A civil war erupts and East Pakistan breaks away to become the independent state of Bangladesh.

(Thursday 12 November 1970)

11.30 a.m.

Mohammed Bouazizi pours a can of petrol over himself and sets it alight. A street vendor in the Tunisian town of Sidi Bouzid, he had been harassed by the authorities who had also confiscated his wares. His action leads to wide-scale anti-government protests, which force the resignation of President Zine El Abidine Ben Ali. The 'Arab Spring' spreads to other countries such as Egypt, Yemen and Libya.

(Friday 17 December 2010)

11.35 a.m.

Earl Mountbatten's fishing boat leaves the harbour at Mullaghmore in County Sligo, Ireland. On board the *Shadow V* are members of his family and a local boat boy. 11 minutes later a remote-controlled bomb is set off. The boat is destroyed and the 79-year-old Mountbatten, one of his grandsons, aged 14, and the 15-year-old local boy Paul Maxwell are killed. Another on board, Baroness Brabourne, dies the next day. Mountbatten had been the last Viceroy of India and had overseen the transfer of British colonial power. It is later revealed that he had sympathies for those seeking a united Ireland.

(Monday 27 August 1979)

11.39 a.m.

The space shuttle *Challenger* sends its last radio signal. During its flight to Earth's orbit as part of mission STS-51, the shuttle is destroyed as a result of a major structural failure. Subsequent investigations find an O-ring in one of the booster rockets has failed due to the cold weather. Another shuttle is lost in 2003 and all are retired in 2011.

(Tuesday 28 January 1986)

11.40 a.m.

Queen Victoria leaves Buckingham Palace on her way to Hyde Park. She is to attend the state opening of the Great Exhibition, which is being held in a specially built structure of glass and steel known as the Crystal Palace. The biggest building in the world is aptly (given the year) 1,851ft long. The Exhibition receives 6 million visitors – almost 30 per cent of the population of Britain – during the five and a half months it is open. An 84-year-old fisherwoman from Cornwall, Mary Kelynack, earns fame for walking 300 miles from Penzance to London to see it. London's Lord Mayor gave her a sovereign, to which she cried and said: 'Now I shall be able to get back.'

(Thursday 1 May 1851)

11.47 a.m.

Police are called to Jill Dando's house in Fulham in London. The TV presenter has been shot. A suspect, Barry George, is convicted of her murder but is later cleared. Ironically, Dando presented the *Crimewatch* programme for the BBC, but her murderer is not brought to justice.

(Monday 26 April 1999)

11.50 a.m.

French artillery open fire on allied positions at Waterloo. The battle sees three armies on the field: the French under Napoleon Bonaparte, the Prussians under Field Marshal Blücher, and the Anglo-Allied Army commanded by the Duke of Wellington. The fighting lasts all day until Napoleon is defeated. Wellington describes the battle as 'the nearest run thing you ever saw in your life'. The victory at Waterloo is immediately celebrated in Britain and many towns see features and streets named after the battle. Napoleon is captured and sent into exile on the South Atlantic island of St Helena, where he dies in 1821.

(Sunday 18 June 1815)

MIDDAY TO 12.59 P.M.

12.00 p.m.

The English Army reach the Tor Wood at Bannockburn. English King Edward II has brought a large force to Scotland to prevent the fall of Stirling Castle. Robert the Bruce has brought a smaller army to stop Edward's approach. In an initial skirmish, the unarmoured Bruce is attacked by a lance-bearing English knight. Bruce rises in his stirrups and brings an axe down onto the knight's head. The incident provides a fillip for the Scots Army, who fight a pitched battle the next day, inflicting the worst defeat on an English Army since 1066. Edward II flees the field, narrowly avoiding capture. Bannockburn is not the end of Scotland's War of Independence, but is a major event along the way.

(Sunday 23 June 1314)

12.00 p.m.

A rowing boat leaves the sailing ship *Duke* and heads for the island off the coast of Chile where a Scotsman called Alexander Selkirk has been living in self-imposed isolation for four years and four months. Selkirk had been worried about the seaworthiness of the ship he was on and had refused to travel any further. Deposited on the island, he regretted his decision as soon as he saw the ship departing. The boat that lands on Juan Fernández Island finds a figure wearing animal skins, a goatskin cap, and sporting a beard. Selkirk's tale is used as inspiration by Daniel Defoe for his novel *Robinson Crusoe*. Selkirk is buried at sea after dying on board a Royal Navy ship in 1721.

(Tuesday 1 February 1709)

12.00 p.m.

Britain's last land battle begins. The Battle of Culloden is fought between the Jacobite army of Bonnie Prince Charlie and the government forces led by the Duke of Cumberland. The battle is a disaster for the prince's ambitions of restoring a Catholic-Stuart monarchy. It is over in less than an hour. The Jacobites lose 2,500 killed in the battle and its immediate aftermath. Government losses number around fifty.

(Wednesday 16 April 1746)

12.00 p.m.

The lighthouse relief vessel SS *Herperus* reaches Eilean Mor, one of the Flannan Isles in the Outer Hebrides. The relief crew find no sign of the three lighthouse keepers. A prepared meal sits uneaten, the clock on the wall is stopped and there is damage to some of the structures on the island. The mystery of the keepers' disappearance is never solved, although the lighthouse superintendent's view that a freak wave took the men to their deaths is the most plausible.

(Wednesday 26 December 1900)

12.00 p.m.

Over 100 troops have reported sick at Fort Riley, a US Army base in Kansas. The first was a cook, Albert Gitchell, who had a high temperature, severe headache, and respiratory difficulties. The infection quickly spreads around the world, with its first major outbreak in Europe, as troops are shipped overseas to take part in the First World War. Estimates suggest that up to 50 million people die of 'Spanish Flu' and that one in four of the global population are infected. More American troops die of the illness than in combat during the war.

(Monday 11 March 1918)

12.00 p.m.

After the excavation of some steps, Howard Carter spots the top of a door displaying the seal of a royal necropolis. Carter is searching for the tomb of Tutankhamun in Egypt's Valley of the Kings when he makes this discovery. He later reveals: 'I needed all my self-control to keep from battering down the door there and then.' Further excavation reveals extraordinary treasures from a tomb that is unique in being virtually untouched in over 3,000 years. Over 3,500 objects are found including jewellery, furniture and chariots. Four shrines, a stone sarcophagus and

12.00 p.m.: Entrance to the tomb of Tutankhamun is found. (Bjørn Christian Tørrissen)

three coffins protect the mummified remains of Tutankhamun. The ancient ruler wears a golden mask of extraordinary beauty.

(Saturday 4 November 1922)

12.00 p.m.

A US Army Air Force major announces that a 'flying disk' has been found. A local newspaper's headline states: 'RAAF Captures Flying Saucer On Ranch In Roswell Region' (RAAF being Roswell Army Air Field). The next day it is announced that the object was a weather balloon and not an alien craft. The 'Roswell incident' becomes the topic of much discussion by ufologists.

(Tuesday 8 July 1947)

12.00 p.m.

Central London hears a sound never to be repeated: The Beatles playing in public. The Fab Four play on the roof of their Apple building in Saville Row for just under three quarters of an hour until they are stopped by the police. Film of the short concert shows excited and curious people on the streets trying to get a better view. The Beatles break up a year later.

(Thursday 30 January 1969)

12.00 p.m.

While digging a well for his village a Chinese farmer hits a solid object. The object is made of terracotta and turns out to be a life-size figure of a soldier. Archaeological excavations reveal underground pits containing a virtual army of similar figures, up to 8,000 in number. The carved figures, dating from 210 BC, are lined up in one direction, guarding the tomb of the First Emperor of China. The site becomes a major tourist attraction.

(Friday 29 March 1974)

12.02 p.m.

The first band to play at Live Aid start the London concert with 'Rockin' all over the world'. Esteemed rockers Status Quo play two more songs before being followed on stage by the Style Council. £150 million is raised from the London and Philadelphia concerts for aid projects in Africa.

(Saturday 13 July 1985)

12.10 p.m.

Football's World Cup goes missing. It has been stolen while on display at Westminster's Methodist Central Hall. The Jules Rimet trophy is missing for a week until it is found in South London. Pickles, a 4-year-old mongrel dog, becomes a celebrity for his part in the recovery. He is given a year's free supply of dog meat and a film contract. His owner receives enough reward money to buy a house, where Pickles is later buried after dying in a freak accident involving a tree branch and his choker lead.

(Sunday 20 March 1966)

12.10 p.m.

A mortar shell lands in the busy marketplace in Sarajevo. Sixty-eight civilians are killed. Serbian forces are blamed for the atrocity. A similar attack is made on the same place a year and a half later, which results in NATO carrying out aerial bombing on Serbian targets. This leads to the Dayton Peace Accord, which ends the war in 1995. In total almost 100,000 people are killed in the Bosnian war.

(Saturday 5 February 1994)

12.15 p.m.

King Wilhelm I enters the Hall of Mirrors in the palace of Versailles. Proclamations are made re-establishing the German Empire, with Wilhelm as emperor. Germany had inflicted a humiliating military defeat on France at Sedan. French emperor Napoleon III surrendered and was captured along with tens of thousands of his troops. The unified Germany grows into a powerful nation, however the Empire only lasts until the First World War when Wilhelm II abdicates. The treaty formally ending that war between the Allies and Germany is signed in the same room in Versailles in 1919.

(Wednesday 18 January 1871)

12.20 p.m.

The British Cabinet is told by the Trades Union Congress that the general strike is over. The strike, started over a reduction in miners' pay and an increase in their working hours, has seen over 1.5 million workers withdraw their labour. The miners continue their strike for a further six months before returning to work, with their conditions reduced.

(Wednesday 12 May 1926)

12.24 p.m.

Ohio National Guardsmen open fire on students at Kent State University. The National Guard has been called in to quell campus protests about America's recent war in Cambodia. Guardsmen, confronted with students throwing rocks and returning tear gas canisters, fire over sixty rounds. Four students are killed and nine injured, including one who is permanently paralysed.

(Monday 4 May 1970)

12.30 p.m.

The first transatlantic wireless message is received. Guglielmo Marconi hears the signal in Signal Hill, Newfoundland, on equipment he has set up for the experiment. The message is composed of three dots – Morse code for the letter 'S' – and has been sent from Cornwall, 2,000 miles away. Although there is debate over whether such a feat is possible, Marconi becomes famous and is later awarded the Nobel Prize for Physics.

(Thursday 12 December 1901)

12.30 p.m.

In Glasgow's Kelvingrove Art Gallery and Museum, a 22-year-old man throws a lump of stone at Salvador Dali's painting 'Christ of St John of the Cross'. He then tears the canvas with his bare hands. The painting, regarded as the Spanish surrealist painter's masterpiece, is eventually restored and put back on display.

(Saturday 22 April 1961)

12.30 p.m.

President John F. Kennedy is shot while travelling through Dallas, Texas, in an open-topped limousine. He is hit by two bullets and despite being rushed to hospital, is pronounced dead half an hour later. Kennedy was the youngest man to be elected president and the first Roman Catholic. With his youthfulness and glamour he was regarded as offering new hope to millions around the world. His assassination was thought to be the work of a lone gunman, Lee Harvey Oswald, although numerous conspiracy theories propose other alternatives.

(Friday 22 November 1963)

12.30 p.m.

Elvis Presley meets President Richard Nixon. The singer has turned up unexpectedly at the White House to discuss how he can help in the fight against drugs. Presley had revolutionised popular music, selling millions of records and providing inspiration to countless musicians. He died in 1977 after a period of prescription drug abuse.

(Monday 21 December 1970)

12.39 p.m.

The *New York Times* receives a telegrammed message that Robert Peary has reached the North Pole. The message starts: 'I have the pole, April 6th'. The previous year another American, Frederick Cook, had claimed to be first. Both Cook's and Peary's claims are subjected to doubt and criticism for not providing enough scientific evidence. The situation encourages Norwegian Roald Amundsen to be extra cautious with his recording of geographical measurements on his journey to the South Pole in 1912.

(Monday 6 September 1909)

12.45 p.m.

A proclamation declaring Ireland a republic is read out on the steps of Dublin's General Post Office. The uprising has seen rebels securing several of the city's major buildings. The British administration declares martial law and troops are rushed to quell the rebellion. Fierce fighting, which includes artillery being used inside the city, leads to over 400 deaths. Heavily outnumbered, the rebels surrender after a week. Fifteen are later executed. The Irish Free State is established in 1922 following a civil war.

(Easter Monday 24 April 1916)

12.50 p.m.

Climbers George Mallory and Sandy Irvine are sighted near the top of Mount Everest. It is the last time they are seen alive. Mallory's body is found in 1999 but Irvine's remains undiscovered. Whether they died on the way down, or while ascending, is not ascertained. Hope remains that if either of the pair's two cameras is found, the mystery may be solved. One indication that they may have been first to climb the world's highest mountain is that a photograph of Mallory's wife is not on his person, a photo he promised he'd leave on the summit. Mallory was once asked why he wanted to climb Everest, to which he answered: 'Because it's there.'

(Sunday 8 June 1924)

12.52 pm

The Irish Mail train from London to Holyhead collides with goods trucks outside Abergele in Wales. The trucks have been allowed to roll down the tracks towards the oncoming train. Some of the trucks are loaded with gallons of paraffin, which ignites on impact. One local woman who goes to help urges a passenger to get out of the train. She is told to mind her own business. Thirty-three are killed in the inferno. It is the worst railway disaster up to that point.

(Thursday 20 August 1868)

12.59 p.m.

President Bill Clinton begins his testimony in a grand jury criminal investigation. Beleaguered over his conduct regarding White House intern Monica Lewinsky, the president faces questions in the Map Room in the White House. He is the first president to be in this position. He later goes on television to admit to having a relationship that he had previously denied. His statement of seven months previously 'I did not have sexual relations with that woman, Miss Lewinsky', becomes the memorable soundbite of his presidency.

(Monday 17 August 1998)

1.00 P.M. TO 1.59 P.M.

1.00 p.m.

Mount Vesuvius erupts, producing a large vertical cloud of ash and rock. The cloud rises to a height of over 20 miles before collapsing. The ensuing torrent of hot gases and ash overwhelms the nearby towns of Herculaneum and Pompeii. While some of the population are able to escape, many are overcome. Some of the victims' bodies are encased and only discovered in the eighteenth century.

(Tuesday 24 August AD 79)

1.00 p.m.

Oliver Cromwell makes his way to Westminster to be installed as republican Lord Protector of England, Scotland and Ireland. He has played a prominent part in the civil wars fighting on the Parliamentarian side against Charles I's Royalist forces and later against Charles II's. He turned down the offer of becoming king, although he effectively rules as monarch during his five years as lord protector. Cromwell's place in history is assured although his brutal policies earn him a less favourable reputation in some places, particularly in Ireland.

(Friday 16 December 1653)

1.00 p.m.

Robert Burns' funeral takes place in Dumfries. A crowd of 10,000 watch the procession make its way to the graveyard. His wife Jean is unable to attend, having given birth to their son Maxwell earlier that day. The poet and songwriter had suffered from ill health, thought to be heart disease, for many years. He died aged only 37, after composing some of the world's best-loved songs such as 'Auld Lang Syne' and 'Ae Fond Kiss', and the poems 'Tam O'Shanter' and 'To a Mouse'. Burns' memory is toasted every year at Burns Suppers.

(Monday 25 July 1796)

1.00 p.m.

Sammy Woods bowls to W.G. Grace. Grace hits a boundary to reach a century – his 100th – the first time this milestone has been achieved. Regarded as possibly the greatest cricketer ever, Grace had a long and superlative career. He scored 54,896 runs in first-class games and his average was almost forty. Although an amateur, in one year he made over £9,000 and was known for gamesmanship, for which some allowance was made. The 'Old Man' retired from playing aged 66, and died in 1915, after reportedly shaking his fist at a German zeppelin.

(Friday 17 May 1895)

1.05 p.m.

An explosion is heard coming from School Number One in the Russian town of Beslan. The school has been occupied for three days by Chechen terrorists, who have taken over 1,000 hostages, including children and their families. The hostages have been held in the school's gym, where bombs have been hung from the roof and the basketball hoop. The explosion starts a gun battle, as Russian troops assault the school. Over 330 people are killed, including 186 children.

(Friday 3 September 2004)

1.15 p.m.

Admiral Horatio Nelson is shot by a single musket round while on the deck of HMS *Victory*. A French marksman has fired from the rigging of the warship *Redoubtable* during the Battle of Trafalgar. Nelson's wounds are fatal and he dies 3 hours later after hearing that the battle is won. His last words are reportedly: 'Thank God I have done my duty.' He is one of Britain's most renowned military heroes and his victory at Trafalgar is one of the most popular.

(Monday 21 October 1805)

1.20 p.m.: Che Guevara is shot dead. (Museo Che Guevara)

1.15 p.m.

A scuffle starts outside a police station in Sharpeville, South Africa. Policemen open fire on unarmed protestors, who have been taking part in a non-violent march against the apartheid system's pass laws. Sixty-nine people are killed, including ten children. Many are shot in the back as they flee the area. A child runs while holding his jacket up as protection against the bullets. One man is shot after running towards police lines, shouting: 'It's enough, you've shot enough.' The incident leads to the banning of anti-apartheid organisations and their adoption of non-peaceful methods of opposition.

(Monday 21 March 1960)

1.20 p.m.

Che Guevara is shot dead. The Marxist revolutionary had gone to Bolivia to fight alongside communist guerrillas and is executed on the orders of the Bolivian president. He is shot to make it look as though he has been killed in combat, making sure his face is untouched so that he can be easily identified. The Argentinean Guevara had played a large part in the revolution and subsequent Communist government in Cuba, alongside Fidel Castro. His death makes him a martyr and his image continues to be reproduced on items such as t-shirts and posters.

(Monday 9 October 1967)

1.20 p.m.

The Beatles land in America. The pop group, who have seen astonishing success in Great Britain, arrive to a chaotic reception from thousands of fans, some attracted by the promise of a dollar each and a free t-shirt courtesy of the Beatles' US merchandising company. At a press conference on arrival the four Liverpudlians are asked: 'How do you find America?' Drummer Ringo Starr replies: 'Turn left at Greenland.' While in America they play several concerts, meet Cassius Clay, and appear on *The Ed Sullivan Show*. Their first appearance has an audience of over 73 million. Beatlemania has hit America.

(Friday 7 February 1964)

1.20 p.m.

American golfer Doug Sanders tees off on the fourth round of the British Open golf tournament. He ends his round only needing to hit four strokes to win the championship. After a poor approach shot to the eighteenth hole, he putts to within 3ft of the hole. In one of the most agonising moments in sport, he misses his putt. Sanders and Jack Nicklaus come back the next day for an eighteen-hole playoff, which Sanders loses by one shot. Despite success on the American PGA tour, he never wins a major tournament.

(Saturday 11 July 1970)

1.30 p.m.

The chief mate of the British vessel *Dei Gratia* is called to the deck, where he sees a vessel 4 or 5 miles away. The vessel is hailed but no answer is received and a boat is sent across. The mate finds not a soul on board. The ship is the *Mary Celeste* and the reason for the disappearance of the crew and passengers is never discovered. The incident becomes one of the great mysteries of the sea.

(Wednesday 4 December 1872)

1.30 p.m.

The first woman to teach at Paris' Sorbonne University begins her lecture. Marie Curie and her husband Pierre had become reluctantly famous for their scientific discoveries, such as discovering the elements radium and polonium. When awarded the Nobel Prize for Physics in 1903, Marie is the first woman to receive the award. She is greatly affected by the death of Pierre in a road accident in April 1906 but continues her work. She develops radiology machines that are used for X-raying wounded soldiers in the First World War, with Curie herself driving cars containing the machines. With little knowledge available about the dangerous qualities of radioactive material, Curie succumbs to leukaemia in 1934. Her laboratory notebooks are still radioactive to this day.

(Monday 5 November 1906)

1.30 p.m.

Bigfoot is filmed. Two American men film what they claim is the sasquatch in northern California. Their 16mm footage is much deliberated over. Experts are divided as to whether it is a hoax, with a person inside a furry ape suit, or real evidence of a previously unfilmed biped.

(Friday 20 October 1967)

1.40 p.m.

Reformer Henry Hunt addresses the crowd at St Peter's Field, Manchester. Around 80,000 have gathered to show support for political reform. Cavalry from the Manchester and Salford Yeomanry ride into the crowd to arrest Hunt and other leaders. They use sabres to clear their way. Eleven people die in what becomes known as the Peterloo Massacre.

(Monday 16 August 1819)

1.42 p.m.

The SS *Great Eastern* is finally launched. The ship, the brainchild of Isambard Kingdom Brunel, is the largest in the world, at almost 700ft in length. It is so big that there is considerable difficulty in getting it into the water. Brunel is regarded as one of the foremost engineers of his day, being responsible for works such as the Clifton Suspension Bridge in Bristol. In 1859 Brunel collapses from a stroke on the deck of the *Great Eastern* and dies before its maiden voyage. It is a failure as a passenger liner but is used to lay the first permanent transatlantic telegraph cable.

(Sunday 31 January 1858)

1.45 p.m.

American pilot Amelia Earhart climbs out of her aircraft after landing in Ireland. She is the first woman to fly solo across the Atlantic and only the second after Lindbergh. Her hazardous flight was intended to reach Paris but a fuel leak forced her to land early. On landing she asks a local man where she is, to be told: 'In Gallagher's pasture. Have you come far?'

(Saturday 21 May 1932)

1.50 p.m.

The first Briton goes into space. Helen Sharman launches from Baikonur space centre in Kazakhstan in a Russian Soyuz rocket. She spends a week in the *Mir* space station before returning to earth. Sharman had responded to a radio advertisement: 'Astronaut wanted. No experience necessary.'

(Saturday 18 May 1991)

1.54 p.m.

Two Frenchmen ascend into the skies above Paris in a Montgolfier balloon. It is mankind's first recorded free flight. It follows a demonstration flight made in front of Louis XVI and Marie Antoinette, which saw a sheep, a rooster and a duck rise into the skies and land safely. The first human aeronauts are watched by Benjamin Franklin, the American Ambassador to France, who sees them tip their hats in salute as they float upwards.

(Friday 21 November 1783)

1.55 p.m.

Famed bandleader Glenn Miller takes off from an RAF base near Bedford. The American is to fly to Paris to conduct a Christmas concert for the troops. His plane disappears into fog shortly after takeoff and is never seen again. One theory suggests that Miller was captured by the Germans, while another claims that his plane was accidentally hit by jettisoned bombs from RAF Lancasters over the Channel.

(Friday 15 December 1944)

2.00 P.M. TO 2.59 P.M.

2.00 p.m.

A Swiss tourist crosses the River Thames to see a play at London's Globe Theatre. He relates seeing a performance of *Julius Caesar*. It is the first of William Shakespeare's plays to be performed there. Although there are claims that the works are not his, Shakespeare is responsible for some of the English language's greatest works and many of the phrases he writes remain in common usage. It is a sign of his literary genius that his works continue to be interpreted and performed five centuries later.

(Friday 21 September 1599)

2.00 p.m.

King Charles I is beheaded. The Stuart king had been arrested and ousted from power following the Civil Wars. Charles' belief in the superiority of the monarch and his right to rule had been resisted by Parliamentarians. He was found guilty of high treason. His son, Charles II, becomes king following the Restoration in 1660.

(Tuesday 30 January 1649)

2.00 p.m.

Charles Darwin boards the survey ship HMS *Beagle*. The 22-year-old naturalist is embarking on a five-year voyage that will take him to the coastlines of South America and then around the world. He collects thousands of samples and makes observations that help form an important part of his Theory of Evolution, which is espoused in his work *On the Origin of Species by means of Natural Selection, or the Preservation of Favoured Races in the Struggle of Life*, which is published over twenty years later. Darwin is not the only person to suggest that evolution is by

2.00 p.m.: Charles Darwin boards the *Beagle*. (James Cameron)

natural selection but his theories receive the most attention. Darwinism remains a controversial subject in some countries.

(Tuesday 27 December 1831)

2.00 p.m.

A US patent application is filed for a system of transmitting multiple messages along telegram lines. Part of the application refers to 'transmitting vocal or other sounds telegraphically'. Three weeks later the patent is granted to the applicant, a Scotsman called Alexander Graham Bell. A few days later he makes the first-ever telephone call when he summons his assistant, Thomas Watson, by saying 'Mr Watson, come here, I want you' on an experimental line set up in a Boston house. Bell becomes a wealthy man as a result of his invention, although he faces accusations that his initial apparatus had used a critical element derived from another inventor, Elisha Gray. When Bell is buried, the Bell telephone system in North America is switched off for 1 minute.

(Monday 14 February 1876)

2.00 p.m.

A Russian schooner is seen off the coast near the Yorkshire town of Whitby. In a force 8 gale the *Dimitry* makes it into the harbour but is destroyed later that night. On a visit a few years later, the Irish author Bram Stoker notes down the details and then uses them in a novel he is writing. In a dramatic passage set in Whitby a Russian ship called the *Demeter* arrives during a storm, its only occupant appearing to be a dead man tied to the wheel. As the ship runs aground a black dog is seen leaping onto shore. The novel is published in 1897 and titled *Dracula*.

(Saturday 24 October 1885)

2.00 p.m.

Radio Teheran finishes broadcasting a fatwā by Ayatollah Khomeini. The decree urges Muslims to kill the author and publishers of the book *The Satanic Verses*. Author Salman Rushdie goes into hiding. Six men are shot by police during a demonstration about the book in Pakistan. More die, including the book's Japanese translator, and others are injured, including one Muslim bomber who accidentally blows himself up in London. Nine years later the Iranian government discourages anyone from carrying out the fatwā, and Rushdie comes out of hiding.

(Tuesday 14 February 1989)

2.17 p.m.

An experiment takes place that proves Albert Einstein's general theory of relativity. On the island of Principe off the west coast of Africa, photographs are taken of stars in the Hyades cluster during a solar eclipse. When compared to photographs taken earlier in the year, they show that light waves have been bent by the Sun. Einstein becomes an international figure as a result of the experiment. His theory is incomprehensible to most, and when forced, he sums it up in one sentence: 'Time and space and gravitation have no separate existence from matter.' Einstein becomes a byword for intellectual ingenuity and he is regarded as truly earning the label 'genius'.

(Thursday 29 May 1919)

2.18 p.m.

An airliner carrying members of a Uruguayan rugby team takes off from

Mendoza in Argentina. It is heading towards Santiago in Chile. The plane cannot fly higher than the highest peak in the Andes and it crashes 11,500ft up in the mountains. An expedition by some of the survivors to walk out to get help is successful and after ten weeks, sixteen survivors are rescued. The joy at their survival is tempered with revulsion when it is revealed that with food running out they ate the flesh of their dead companions.

(Friday 13 October 1972)

2.22 p.m.

Beams cross in the Large Hadron Collider, causing particle collisions for the first time. The collider is the biggest scientific apparatus ever built. It is a particle accelerator, 17 miles in circumference, situated under the ground at the CERN laboratory in Switzerland. It is designed to answer questions about the origins of the universe. There is much speculation about whether operating the machine will cause the Earth to fall into a black hole. So far, no such incident has occurred.

(Monday 23 November 2009)

2.23 p.m.

World Champion Niki Lauda's Ferrari crashes at Germany's Nürburgring race track. His Formula 1 car immediately starts to burn. Other drivers stop to help pull the trapped Austrian from his blazing car. Despite suffering horrendous injuries, Lauda returns to Grand Prix racing six weeks later. He loses that year's championship to Britain's James Hunt after withdrawing from the final race in Japan over safety issues. Lauda says: 'My life is worth more than a title'. He wins the championship the following year.

(Sunday 1 August 1976)

2.34 p.m.

The jury returns to the Old Bailey's Court Number 1 to deliver its verdict in the trial of Jeremy Thorpe and three other men. Thorpe was until recently the leader of the Liberal Party. He resigned the leadership under a cloud of allegations that centred on the attempted murder of Norman Scott, said to be Thorpe's lover. Thorpe is acquitted but his political career is over.

(Friday 22 June 1979)

2.35 p.m.

The first bombs of the Second World War to fall on the British Isles are released. A German bomber squadron is attacking Royal Navy ships berthed at Rosyth, close to the Forth Bridge outside Edinburgh. Royal Air Force Spitfires shoot the first bomber down over Britain soon afterwards.

(Monday 16 October 1939)

2.45 p.m.

Royal Navy Lieutenant Stanley Worth arrives at a house in Portsmouth to attend a séance by medium Helen Duncan. Worth is visited by the spirit of a dead aunt, despite all his aunts still being alive. He informs the police, who attend a later séance where a torch is shone on Duncan attempting to hide a length of white cloth that she had used to simulate the appearance of spirits. At their subsequent trial Duncan and three others are found guilty under the Witchcraft Act of 1735, with Duncan sent to prison for nine months. She is mistakenly assumed to have been tried as a witch, but is in fact tried under a section of the act that pertains to pretending to be able to summon the spirits of those deceased.

(Friday 14 January 1944)

2.46 p.m.

A woman called Ann Elizabeth Hodges is sleeping on her couch when she is hit by a falling meteorite. The 8½lb rock comes through the ceiling of her house in Talladega County, Alabama. The meteorite had been seen by many people as it trailed across the afternoon sky. Mrs Hodges is the only recorded person to have been injured by an extraterrestrial object. The incident brings her little good fortune as she and husband separate in 1964, both wishing the incident and its attendant fame had not happened.

(Tuesday 30 November 1954)

2.46 p.m.

A tremor occurs 80 miles east of Sendai in Japan. The initial earthquake measures 9.0 magnitude and is the biggest Japan has ever experienced. Tsunamis, some of which are 40m high, swamp parts of the coastline. Towns disappear off the map and there are fears that a nuclear power station could go into meltdown. Over 19,009 people are declared missing or confirmed dead to date.

(Friday 11 March 2011)

2.47 p.m.

A gate is opened to allow more Liverpool fans into the Hillsborough football ground for the FA Cup semi-final against Nottingham Forest. The influx into an already crowded enclosure causes a crush. Fans are unable to escape onto the pitch because of metal fencing barriers. Over 750 are injured and ninety-six are killed in Britain's worst sporting disaster. The police are heavily criticised over allegations of an attempted cover-up.

(Saturday 15 April 1989)

3.00 P.M. TO 3.59 P.M.

3.00 p.m.

Jesus of Nazareth dies. He is crucified in Calvary after being sentenced by Roman governor Pontius Pilate. His strong religious and moral teachings are an inspiration to his disciples, who go out to spread the word to the rest of the world. Jesus' life is the subject of much discussion as to which of the stories told in the Bible are historic events or simple allegories. Born a Jew, Jesus' death gives life to the Christian religion.

(Friday 3 April AD 33)

3.00 p.m.

A large audience has gathered in Paris' Palace of the Institute for a joint meeting of the Academy of Fine Arts and the Academy of Sciences. They are gathered to hear details of a new process of creating photographic images. Devised by Louis Daguerre, who is too ill to present it himself, the process involves capturing images on copper plates coated with silver. Many 'daguerreotypes' are created, although they are eventually replaced as the commonly adopted means of recording images.

(Monday 19 August 1839)

3.00 p.m.

Trading ends on the New York Stock Exchange following a day of frenetic trading. A record 12.9 million shares have been traded on what becomes known as 'Black Thursday.' *The Times* newspaper calls it 'a Niagara of liquidation'. The situation does not improve with 'Black Tuesday' the following week, which sees panic selling on a huge scale. The world's economy soon plunges into the Great Depression that lasts up to twelve years.

(Thursday 24 October 1929)

3.00 p.m.

The Post Office Tower opens to the public. The building is over 600ft high and becomes a new landmark on the London skyline. Despite its prominence, it is not included on Ordnance and Survey maps for security reasons. It has a rotating restaurant on the top, initially operated by Butlins. In 1971, the tower is a target for the IRA, who explode a bomb in the toilets on the thirty-third floor.

(Thursday 19 May 1966)

3.00 p.m.

The men's long jump final starts at the 1968 Mexico City Olympics. On his first jump, American Bob Beamon lands 29ft 2½in from the jump-off block. He has broken the existing record by an incredible distance of 21¾in. His world record stands for twenty-three years and the Olympic record remains to this day. British long jumper Lynn Davies said: 'We were all completely demoralised by that first effort of Bob Beamon's. I knew I would never be able to match that. What would have been the use?'

(Friday 18 October 1968)

3.00 p.m.

Shares in British Telecom are traded for the first time. The telecommunications part of the Post Office has been privatised by the Conservative government in a policy designed to raise revenue and increase share ownership among the population. Over 2 million new shareholders are created, many tempted by the government's buy-one-get-two-free offer. The share price rises immediately, giving a 30 per cent profit on the first day. Opponents criticise the sale as being an incompetent giveaway. Over forty other state-owned industries are sold off, including gas, electricity, airports, airlines, railways, steel, and water.

(Monday 3 December 1984)

3.04 p.m.

An Airspeed Ambassador aircraft carrying the Manchester United football team begins its third take-off attempt from Munich-Riem Airport. Manchester United had chartered the aircraft to take them to and from a European Cup match in Yugoslavia. The take-off ends in disaster as the plane crashes off the end of the runway in snowy conditions. Twenty-three passengers die as a result, including eight of the team. Northern Irish goalkeeper Harry Gregg helps pull survivors from the wreckage.

(Thursday 6 February 1958)

3.09 p.m.

A 500lb bomb explodes in the Northern Ireland market town of Omagh. Twenty-nine people are killed and over 200 injured in the worst incident in the history of the Troubles. Among the dead are Avril Monaghan – who is pregnant with twins – her mother, and her 18-month-old daughter. The sense of aggrieved loss is exacerbated by the signing of the Good Friday agreement four months previously. The Real IRA claim responsibility and apologise for the deaths of 'civilians'.

(Saturday 15 August 1998)

3.10 p.m.

Suffragette Emily Davison runs into the path of the king's horse Anmer in the Epsom Derby. It is not known if she meant suicide or was only attempting to interrupt the race. Four days later she dies of her injuries. The jockey, Herbert Jones, is traumatised by the incident for the rest of his life and kills himself almost forty years later. The Suffragette movement aims to secure suffrage – voting rights – for women. It is not until 1928 that all women are given the vote.

(Wednesday 4 June 1913)

3.11 p.m.

Glasgow Airport comes under terrorist attack. The attempt to ram the airport building with a SUV filled with gas canisters is foiled. The two terrorists are arrested after being tackled by bystanders. One of them, baggage handler John Smeaton, becomes an international celebrity for his heroism. He is interviewed on television after the incident and his expression of defiance makes him an Internet sensation: 'Glasgow doesnae accept this, if you come tae Glasgow, we'll set about you.'

(Saturday 30 June 2007)

3.12 p.m.

The world's first jet airliner enters service. A de Havilland Comet G-ALYP operated by the British Overseas Aircraft Corporation (BOAC) takes off from London for Johannesburg. A BOAC advert on the day of the return flight reads: 'The Comet is quiet and free from vibration. Travel fatigue is reduced to the vanishing point.' Unfortunately metal fatigue isn't, and Comets suffer a series of fatal accidents, one of them involving G-ALYP. As the manufacturer tackles a redesign, Britain's lead in jet air transportation is lost for good. The American Boeing 707 secures orders from airlines including BOAC.

(Friday 2 May 1952)

3.15 p.m.

The runners and riders start off in the Grand National. One of the horses is Red Rum, who has won the National twice and come second twice, but isn't seen as the favourite. In front of an ecstatic crowd and live television audience, the 12-year-old races home the winner – by 25 lengths. After the race a bookmaker says: 'We've lost a quarter of a million and I simply don't care.' Red Rum becomes a national treasure and is honoured by being buried beside the Aintree winning post.

(Saturday 2 April 1977)

3.30 p.m.

Joseph Merrick is found dead. Known as the 'Elephant Man' because of the disfigurement of his body, he has been living in rooms in London Hospital funded by public well-wishers. Merrick's condition worsened through his life and it was in the later period that he received more civility and understanding. When he was younger, he had to appear in freak shows to earn money. His death is first put down to asphyxiation (his head blocking his windpipe), although Frederick Treves, a surgeon who has befriended him, asserts that the reason is a dislocated neck. Merrick had quoted a poem by Isaac Watts in his letters. It starts: 'Tis true my form is something odd, but blaming me is blaming God.'

(Friday 11 April 1890)

3.30 p.m.

Three airliners are blown up by Palestinian terrorists in Jordan. The Popular Front for the Liberation of Palestine had hijacked five aircraft, one of which was reclaimed after an onboard struggle. Another was flown to Cairo where it was destroyed. All passengers are eventually recovered safely. Some of the British child hostages sing a song about being on a hijacked plane to the tune of The Beatles' song 'Yellow Submarine'.

(Saturday 12 September 1970)

3.30 p.m.

Banks close early in order to prepare for D-Day. On the following Monday, Britain's currency will go decimal when a new currency is introduced. A pound is now made up of 100 new pence. Some of Britain's best-known coins, such as tanners, florins and thrupennies eventually leave circulation.

(Wednesday 11 February 1971)

3.31 p.m.

An airliner piloted by Captain Chesley B. 'Sully' Sullenberger ditches in the Hudson River in New York. The Airbus A320 had taken off from LaGuardia Airport and flown through a flock of Canada geese. The flight only lasts 6 minutes, with half of that time spent with no engine power. Captain Sullenberger, the last to leave the half-submerged plane, is later praised for his actions in bringing the aircraft down in a successful ditching. All on board are saved.

(Thursday 15 January 2009)

3.32 p.m.

Prohibition ends in America. The state of Utah becomes the thirty-sixth state to ratify the 21st Amendment, which allows the manufacture and sale of intoxicating liquors. Alcohol consumption has reduced and deaths from drink-related ailments has also fallen but Prohibition has proven to be unpopular. Prohibition's other effect has been the rise in power of underworld 'bootlegging' gangsters able to amass enough money to buy political influence. Not all states are so keen to end Prohibition. Mississippi abolishes it in 1966.

(Tuesday 5 December 1933)

3.33 p.m.

Parliament begins a debate on whether or not Britain should join the European Community. After 7 hours of discussion a vote is taken. The 'Ayes' have it, with 356 MPs for and 244 against. Public opinion in Britain is deeply divided on the issue. A French newspaper states: 'Britain is no longer an island.'

(Thursday 28 October 1971)

3.36 p.m.

Evel Knievel launches his Skycycle X2. He is attempting to ride a rocket sled over the Snake River Canyon. Viewers watch live on television as the parachutes come out too early and the rocket slows down dramatically before drifting gently backwards, then down to the bottom of the canyon out of sight. Knievel's failure doesn't stop him in his stunt-riding efforts however. The next year, he jumps over thirteen London buses on a motorbike. Knievel clears the line of buses but his landing ends badly, and he falls off. He vows never to make another jump. Five months later he jumps fourteen buses in Ohio.

(Sunday 8 September 1974)

3.40 p.m.

There is a new shape in the skies as Concorde flies for the first time. Ex-Spitfire pilot Raymond Baxter commentates on the occasion for live television and his comment 'She flies, she flies!' sums up the national interest and enthusiasm for the sleek craft.

(Sunday 2 March 1969)

3.42 p.m.

James Bulger is led out of New Strand Shopping Centre in Bootle, Merseyside, by two older boys. They are Robert Thompson and Jon Venables, both aged 10. They torture and then kill the 2-year-old toddler on a railway line. They are found guilty of murder and released eight years afterwards. Venables is later found guilty of downloading child pornography is and sent back to prison in 2010.

(Friday 12 February 1993)

3.50 p.m.: The first boat arrives at Ellis Island. (National Archives)

3.50 p.m.

The SS *Nevada* arrives in New York. The next day its passengers are the first to enter the United States through the immigration centre on Ellis Island. The first to be registered is 17-year-old Annie Moore from Cork in Ireland. She receives a $10 gold coin to mark the occasion. Moore says that she'll never part with it, but family legend has it that her father spent the money on drink. It is estimated that by 1890 two fifths of the Irish population have emigrated. Much emigration took place following the famine of the 1840s.

(Thursday 31 December 1891)

3.50 p.m.

A de Havilland 110 jet breaks up in flight during the Farnborough Airshow in front of 120,000 people. Wreckage falls into the packed crowd, killing twenty-nine people. The pilot, John Derry, who'd become the first Briton to fly faster than the speed of sound four years earlier, and his observer Anthony Richards are also killed. The display continues and a bigger crowd of 140,000 attend the show the next day.

(Saturday 6 September 1952)

3.55 p.m.

In Derry, two men are hit by the first bullets fired by British Paratroops on Bloody Sunday. Thirteen civilians are killed and eighteen are injured in the incident, which contributes to the ill feeling prevalent in the Northern Ireland Troubles. At the time British troops claim they had been fired on first but an enquiry in 2010 finds that this is untrue and all those killed were innocent. By the end of the Troubles, over 3,500 people have been killed.

(Sunday 30 January 1972)

3.57 p.m.

Royal Navy submarine HMS *Conqueror* fires three torpedoes at the Argentinean cruiser *General Belgrano*. The ship sinks within 2 hours with over 300 Argentine sailors killed. There is immediate controversy over whether it should have been attacked or not, due to it sailing outside a British-imposed exclusion zone around the Falkland Islands. The conflict ends six weeks later with a British invasion force reaching Port Stanley and the Argentine garrison surrendering.

(Sunday 2 May 1982)

4.00 P.M. TO 4.59 P.M.

4.00 p.m.

Shortly after spotting the English coastline, sailors of the Spanish Armada take Mass. The Spanish force consists of over 120 ships carrying around 20,000 troops. Admiral Lord Howard leads his fleet out of Plymouth and engages the Spanish in the English Channel for a week. A possibly apocryphal story tells of how Francis Drake, one of Howard's admirals, continued his game of bowls on Plymouth Hoe upon hearing news of the Armada's arrival. Off Flanders, the English use of fire ships and a fortunate storm forces the Armada to flee. The Spanish sail north and around Scotland and Ireland, where high seas and further bad weather see another thirty-five vessels lost. Only sixty-five ships make it back to Spanish waters later that year.

(Friday 29 July 1588)

4.00 p.m.

Isaac Newton returns home to be presented with two mathematical problems. He stays up most of the night until he finds the solutions to Bernouilli's Programma. It is an example of Newton's renowned mental abilities, which have seen him formulate a theory of universal gravitation. His three laws of motion have an enormous impact on the development of engineering and science. Newton is reported to have pondered the effects of gravity after seeing an apple fall to the ground, although contrary to popular myth, it may not have fallen on his head.

(Friday 29 January 1697)

4.00 p.m.

A couple returning to London from a holiday in the north of Scotland are driving past Loch Ness when they see something crossing the road ahead of them. They describe it as being dark elephant grey in colour and around 30ft in length. The driver, George Spicer, says it was 'the nearest approach to a dragon or prehistoric animal that I have ever seen in my life.' It is just one sighting of what is termed the Loch Ness Monster. The creature has intrigued locals and visitors alike for centuries, dating back to St Columba in the sixth century. English writer G.K. Chesterton wrote: 'Many a man has been hanged on less evidence than there is for the Loch Ness Monster'.

(Saturday 22 July 1933)

4.00 p.m.

Bombs rain down on the *Torrey Canyon*. The supertanker has run aground off the Cornish coast and its cargo of 119,000 tonnes of crude oil has been spilling into the sea for over ten days. Royal Navy and Royal Air Force jets drop high-explosive bombs to try to sink the oil tanker and set the oil on fire. The tanker eventually sinks and the oil is dispersed by the weather.

(Tuesday 28 March 1967)

4.00 p.m.

A new era in science begins as Dolly the sheep is born. She is the first animal to be cloned from an adult cell. Her birth is not announced until the following year when research findings are published by scientists from the Roslin Institute. She immediately becomes the centre of worldwide interest. Dolly develops arthritis and then in 2003 a scan detects tumours on her lungs. A decision is made to prevent any further suffering and she is put down. Dolly, who was named after Dolly Parton as the initial cell was taken from a mammary gland, is placed on display in Edinburgh's National Museum of Scotland.

(Friday 5 July 1996)

4.05 p.m.

The 'Birmingham Six' are released at the Old Bailey court in London. The men had been convicted of carrying out bombing attacks on two Birmingham pubs in 1974. Twenty-one people had been killed in the bombings and scores more were injured. The men had served sixteen years behind bars. Lord Devlin described the miscarriage of justice (along with those of the 'Guildford Four' and the 'Maguire Seven') as 'the greatest disasters that have shaken British justice in my time'.

(Thursday 14 March 1991)

4.06 p.m.

A worker in a London law firm emails his girlfriend a smutty joke. She replies and their ensuing sex-related email conversation is then forwarded by him to some of his male friends. It then cascades outwards, around the world, creating an Internet meme (a sudden fad). The boyfriend and other workers are suspended, and the woman goes into hiding. It is an example of the power of the Internet to communicate in ways and at speeds previously unimaginable.

(Thursday 7 December 2000)

4.08 p.m.

Margaret Thatcher arrives at No. 10 Downing Street from Buckingham Palace where the queen has invited her to form a government. Thatcher's time in office sees bitter struggles over the coal miners' and other trades unions, as well as war with Argentina over the Falkland Islands. Britain's first female prime minister quotes from St Francis of Assisi on the doorstep of her new home: 'Where there is discord, may we bring harmony. Where there is error, may we bring truth. Where there is doubt, may we bring faith. And where there is despair, may we bring hope.'

(Friday 4 May 1979)

4.10 p.m.

Mussolini is executed by machine-gun fire. Italy's self-styled Il Duce (The Leader) had been making his way to Switzerland with German troops when their convoy is stopped by Italian partisans. The following day Mussolini is hanged upside down from the roof of a Milan garage. His fascist party had been in power for over twenty years. Assuming that the war would be over quickly, in 1940 he declared war on Britain and France. Mussolini had wanted to restore Italy's position as a great European state.

(Saturday 28 April 1945)

4.14 p.m.: Nelson Mandela. (Creative Commons/South Africa, The Good News)

4.14 p.m.

Nelson Mandela arrives at the gates of Victor-Verster Prison in Paarl. The 71-year-old is free after twenty-seven years' incarceration. Jailed for treason and sabotage, he has spent most of his imprisonment on Robben Island, doing hard labour. He becomes President of South Africa after a transition of power from the minority rule of South Africa's whites to a democratic, multi-racial state.

(Sunday 11 February 1990)

4.15 p.m.

Skiffle group The Quarrymen start playing at a garden fête at St Peter's church in Woolton, Liverpool. During their performance a 15-year-old schoolboy called Paul McCartney arrives to see them singing a song by The Dell Vikings called 'Come Go With Me'. Afterwards he is introduced to the Quarrymen's singer, John Lennon, and plays several rock and roll tunes for him. Lennon is suitably impressed and a few days later McCartney is asked to join the group. One of the gravestones in the church's graveyard commemorates an Eleanor Rigby.

(Saturday 6 July 1957)

4.15 p.m.

Valerie Solanas meets up with artist Andy Warhol at his New York studio. Minutes later she pulls out a revolver and shoots him. He is seriously injured and has to have his spleen removed. Warhol eventually recovers and Solanas is jailed, although Warhol remains anxious that she might repeat her attack. Warhol dies in 1987, one of the most renowned artists in the Pop Art movement, famous for his paintings of soup cans and screen-printed images of Marilyn Monroe, Elvis and Jacqueline Kennedy.

(Monday 3 June 1968)

4.20 p.m.

In a laboratory in Basel, Switzerland, Albert Hoffman ingests a chemical called lysergic acid diethylamide. He is experimenting on himself in order to find the substance that produced vivid hallucinations the previous Friday when he ingested chemicals through his fingertips. The experiment sees him fear insanity through the frightening visions he sees. At one point a neighbour brings him some milk, and he sees her as a witch wearing a mask. The terrifying changes in his perception of reality eventually diminish and he recovers. The chemical formulation, LSD, forms the basis of the psychedelic 1960s.

(Monday 19 April 1943)

4.22 p.m.

Two trains collide at Chatsworth, Los Angeles. One of the vehicles, a passenger train, has passed through a red light onto a single-track stretch of the railway where it hits a freight train. Twenty-five people are killed and over 100 are injured in one of America's worst rail disasters. An enquiry finds that the driver of the passenger train had sent a text message only seconds before the collision.

(Friday 12 September 2008)

4.23 p.m.

Annie Edson Taylor goes over the Niagara Falls in a barrel. She is the first to complete the stunt and comes away relatively intact with a cut forehead and some bruises. She is removed from the barrel and says

'Nobody ought ever to do that again'. Taylor attempted the feat in order to secure her financial future, but she dies destitute twenty years later.

(Thursday 24 October 1901)

4.30 p.m.

Thomas à Becket, the Archbishop of Canterbury, is murdered in his own cathedral, after falling out with King Henry II. The king is reported to have said 'Will no one rid me of this turbulent priest?' Four knights had arrived earlier in the afternoon to meet Becket, saying they had a message from the king. After a confrontation, he is attacked and killed, the first blow taking the top of his head off. Becket is canonised three years later.

(Tuesday 29 December 1170)

4.30 p.m.

In the second year of the Spanish Civil War, the Basque town of Guernica is attacked by German bombers operating on the side of General Franco's Nationalist forces. Thousands of pounds of bombs fall on the market town, killing hundreds. It inspires Pablo Picasso to paint his most famous work.

(Monday 26 April 1937)

4.30 p.m.

US Marines enter Fidros Square in Baghdad. The marines see a statue of Saddam Hussein and allow Iraqis to use their ropes and sledgehammers to try to bring it down. An American flag is put on the statue's head before being quickly replaced by an Iraqi one. The marines use one of their vehicles to pull the statue over. Shown live on television, it is portrayed as symbolic event in the downfall of Saddam Hussein's regime following the invasion of Iraq. Three weeks later President Bush declares that major combat operations are complete, in front of a banner that reads 'Mission Accomplished'. Despite this, coalition troops face an insurgent campaign amid allegations of inadequate preparation for the post-invasion situation.

(Wednesday 9 April 2003)

4.40 p.m.

Galileo Galilei sees Jupiter through a telescope for the first time. The Italian astronomer notices stars near to the planet, which, after further viewings, give him the evidence to offer a theory that forever changes how the universe is viewed. If objects are orbiting Jupiter, then logic says that not everything in the heavens orbits around the Earth. This view leads to Galileo standing trial by the Inquisition. He is found guilty of heresy and kept under house arrest for the rest of his life. Forced to sign a declaration denying his view that the Earth is mobile, he is rumoured to have said under his breath: 'And yet it moves.'

(Thursday 7 January 1610)

4.40 p.m.

A downpour of heavy rain falls near the Cornish village of Boscastle. Almost an inch of rain is recorded in just 15 minutes. The water surges downhill and flows into the village, breaching the riverbanks. It is estimated that the torrent races at 140 tons per second. Footage shows bystanders watching as cars, trees and other debris rush past them. Remarkably, no one is killed in the flood.

(Monday 16 August 2004)

4.42 p.m.

Air France Concorde F-BTSC begins its take-off run at Paris' Charles De Gaulle Airport. A piece of metal from another airliner on the runway causes a rupture in a petrol tank. Fire breaks out under the left wing. The supersonic airliner is unable to halt its take-off and struggles into the air. Heading for nearby Le Bourget Airport, it stalls and crashes into a hotel. All on board and four on the ground are killed. It is Concorde's first fatal crash and leads to the type's retirement in 2003.

(Tuesday 25 July 2000)

4.48 p.m.

The longest-ever tennis match comes to an end at Wimbledon. American John Isner beats Nicolas Mahut of France in an epic game that has lasted 11 hours and included 980 points and 183 games. The fifth and final set ends 70-68. The beaten Mahut says: 'I thought he would make a mistake. I waited for that moment, and it never came.'

(Thursday 24 June 2010)

4.55 p.m.

Blue Peter goes on air. A baby elephant called Lulu is brought into the studio and in the excitement of live television leaves a puddle of urine and faeces on the floor, on which the keeper slips and falls. Lulu also stands on presenter John Noakes' foot, creating a classic TV moment.

(Thursday 3 July 1969)

5.00 P.M. TO 5.59 P.M.

5.00 p.m.

A committee of Bostonians await a reply from the Massachusetts lieutenant governor regarding three ships carrying tea that are docked in the town's harbour. They wish the ships to be allowed to leave with their cargo of tea still on board. If the ships were unloaded, a tax would have to be paid. The governor does not back the colonists and so the locals take matters into their own hands. Some disguise themselves in 'Indian Dress' and once on board throw the tea chests into the water. The action is part of protests against the British government for its approach to taxation of the colonies. The slogan 'No taxation without representation' is used by the American patriots. The Boston Tea Party is a key moment in the build-up to the War of Independence.

(Thursday 16 December 1773)

5.00 p.m.

The Bastille's inner gates are opened. The notorious Paris prison has been under siege all day by a gathering mob looking to acquire the prison's ammunition supplies. Almost 100 are killed before the governor capitulates. The mob's ensuing chaotic violence results in the governor and others being beheaded and their heads displayed on poles. The storming of the Bastille is recognised later as the symbolic event of the French Revolution, becoming a national day of celebration.

(Tuesday 14 July 1789)

5.00 p.m.

Seventeen slaves are taken to jail on the Caribbean island of Trinidad. A British parliamentary act has abolished slavery, but only for those under the age of 6. Those older are now termed 'apprentices' and have to keep on working for their owners for another six years. A crowd of older men, women and children march to the governor's residence to protest, disappointed that they are still, in effect, slaves. They interrupt his speech with cries of '*Pas de six ans*!' (No six years). It takes another four years for all to be set free.

(Friday 1 August 1834)

5.00 p.m.

Ernest Shackleton gives the order to abandon ship. *Endurance* has been trapped in Antarctic ice for nine months and is now being crushed. Shackleton's exploration expedition is now one of survival. After living on the ice and then setting up camp on the remote Elephant Island, Shackleton leads a small crew in a desperate bid for help. They sail for South Georgia in a boat only 22ft long. The 800-mile journey takes them seventeen days. They then cross a mountain range to reach a Norwegian whaling station. Four months after leaving Elephant Island, Shackleton returns to pick up his men. One of the most remarkable feats of survival is over. After the *Endurance* had sunk, Shackleton told his men: 'Ship and stores have gone, so now we'll go home.'

(Wednesday 27 October 1915)

5.00 p.m.

American athlete Jesse Owens wins the 100m, the first of his four gold medals at the 1936 Berlin Olympics. His achievements come as an embarrassment to the watching Nazi hierarchy. After his victory in the long jump, Owens is immediately congratulated by his German competitor, Lutz Long. Owens later says: 'You can melt down all the medals and cups I have won and they wouldn't be worth the plating on the 24 carat friendship I felt for Lutz Long at that moment.'

(Monday 3 August 1936)

5.00 p.m.

Oswald Mosley is due to speak at a rally of British fascists in the east of London. He is prevented from doing so by a concerted effort of protestors. 100 people are injured in what becomes known as the Battle of Cable Street. One witness said: 'I was moved to tears to see

5.00 p.m.: Jesse Owens wins the 100m. (Unknown)

bearded Jews and Irish Catholic dockers standing up to stop Mosley. I shall never forget that as long as I live, how working-class people could get together to oppose the evil of racism.' The British Union of Fascists sees its support dwindle. It had received backing from Lord Rothermere whose papers the *Daily Mail* and the *Daily Mirror* included headlines such as 'Give the Blackshirts a Helping Hand' in 1934.

(Sunday 4 October 1936)

5.00 p.m.

The Jarrow Crusade arrives at its first stop at Chester-le-Street. 200 unemployed men and their supporters are marching to London to campaign for jobs. Their area has 72 per cent unemployment. The marchers arrive in London after twenty-six days on the road. They receive numerous offers of food and lodgings on the way down, which leads one of the marchers to say: 'I never thought there was so much generosity and good nature in the world.' Their campaign achieves little except the raising of awareness of their plight. Rubbing salt into the wound, the marchers find they have been docked unemployment assistance for the time they have been away. It takes the Second World War to help the Wearside economy.

(Monday 5 October 1936)

5.00 p.m.

The concentration camp at Bergen-Belsen is liberated. It is the first camp to be reached by British troops, who are not prepared for what they encounter. Bergen-Belsen is the camp where Anne Frank has died only weeks before the troops arrive. The Holocaust is the result of the Nazi 'Final Solution' persecution of the Jews, in which six million die. Other groups such as gypsies, homosexuals, Jehovah's Witnesses and resistance fighters are also murdered in the camps.

(Sunday 15 April 1945)

5.00 p.m.

A dead swan is found in the harbour of the Fife village of Cellardyke. The Mute Swan is tested and found to have been infected with H5N1 Avian Flu. It is Britain's first case of the pathogenic virus. Fears of a pandemic are widespread although swift preventative measures by health officials ensure there is no outbreak and no threat to the population.

(Wednesday 29 March 2006)

5.06 p.m.

One of the worst-ever aviation disasters happens in Tenerife, as a KLM Boeing 747, attempting to take off, hits a Pan Am 747 that is taxiing on the runway. The KLM airliner had started its take-off run without clear permission. Fog and the lack of ground radar prevent air traffic control and both of the planes' crews from realising the situation until it is too late. 583 people are killed in the collision and ensuing fire. All on board the KLM plane die.

(Sunday 27 March 1977)

5.10 p.m.

Mahatma Gandhi is walking to a prayer meeting when he is shot dead. The 'father of India' has seen his country become independent, free from the rule of the British Empire. He has advocated non-violent forms of protest, and is on a fast to improve Hindu-Muslim relations when he is killed.

(Friday 30 January 1948)

5.15 p.m.

Britain sees its only prime ministerial assassination. Spencer Perceval is making his way through the Houses of Parliament when he is shot. His murderer is John Bellingham, who wants revenge after not being helped by the government following his arrest and imprisonment in Russia. Perceval's last words are: 'Oh I have been murdered.' Bellingham is found guilty and hanged.

(Monday 11 May 1812)

5.15 p.m.

The final whistle blows at Wembley Stadium and England are World Cup football champions for the first and, so far, only time. They have beaten Germany 4-2 in a keenly contested game. Captain Bobby Moore being hoisted aloft by his teammates with the gold Jules Rimet trophy becomes a lasting symbol of English sporting achievement.

(Saturday 30 July 1966)

5.15 p.m.

Pope John Paul II is shot. While being driven through St Peter's Square in the Vatican City, the head of the Catholic Church is hit four times by a Turkish man, whom the Pope later forgives. John Paul II is beatified in 2011. He had supported his homeland Poland's move towards democratisation through the Solidarity movement.

(Wednesday 13 May 1981)

5.17 p.m.

A session of a special Senate investigation finishes for the day. During the hearing, Senator Joe McCarthy has provoked the ire of lawyer Joseph Welch by alleging that a young lawyer in Welch's firm has communist tendencies. Welch responds by saying: 'Let us not assassinate this lad further, Senator. You have done enough. Have you no sense of decency, sir?' McCarthy's investigations into the supposed infiltration of communists into American life has seen hundreds facing his accusations. Welch's words lead to McCarthy's downfall. He is censured by Congress and dies three years later, a broken man.

(Wednesday 9 June 1954)

5.18 p.m.

Lieutenant Thomas Selfridge becomes the first passenger to die in an aeroplane crash. The army officer is being given a demonstration flight by Orville Wright when the plane suffers a broken propeller. Wright loses control and they plummet to earth from 60ft up. Wright is seriously injured, but recovers. The crash site is a few hundred feet from Arlington Cemetery where Selfridge is later buried.

(Thursday 17 September 1908)

5.30 p.m.

The eighth and final assassination attempt or attack is made on Queen

Victoria. She is leaving Windsor railway station when Scotsman Roderick MacLean fires a revolver at her carriage. He is later found 'not guilty but insane' for the attack and committed to an asylum. The queen is not harmed. The would-be assassin had claimed that all the people in England were against him – shown by them wearing blue – and that the queen, as their representative, was a legitimate target. She is reported to have said: 'It was worth being shot at to see how much one is loved.'

(Thursday 2 March 1882)

5.30 p.m.

The men's 400m final starts at the Paris Olympics. Scottish runner Eric Liddell races ahead and holds on for a famous win, creating new world and Olympic records. He has been preparing for six months since finding out his religious convictions prevent him from taking part in the 100m, due to the heats taking place on a Sunday. Liddell also wins bronze medal in the 200m. He retires from athletics to pursue his calling as a missionary in China, where he was born. He is interned by the Japanese and dies of typhoid in 1945.

(Friday 11 July 1924)

5.30 p.m.

Police raid the home of Rolling Stones guitarist Keith Richards. Amongst his guests are fellow Stones singer Mick Jagger, Jagger's girlfriend Marianne Faithful, and London art gallery owner Robert Fraser. Jagger, Richards and Fraser are all found guilty of drugs offences, although the Stones men's convictions are later quashed on appeal. The police had been tipped off by a drug dealer. Despite rumours, Marianne Faithful was not involved with a Mars bar.

(Sunday 12 February 1967)

5.30 p.m.

An unclaimed National Lottery ticket expires. Worth £9,476,995 it was bought in the Doncaster area for the draw on 6 July of the previous year. It remains the largest unclaimed amount in the National Lottery's history, which started on Saturday 19 November 1994. There is a 1 in 14 million chance of getting the six numbers required for the top prize.

(Tuesday 2 January 1996)

5.30 p.m.

'Canoe man' John Darwin walks into a London police station. He claims to be a missing person and to be suffering from amnesia. The former prison officer disappeared off the coast near Hartlepool in 2002 and was declared dead the following year. In the intervening years he had spent time living secretly next to his own home, as well as using a fake passport to travel abroad. He and his wife are arrested for fraud after the couple are spotted in a photograph on a Panama estate agent's website. They are both jailed.

(Saturday 1 December 2007)

5.35 p.m.

American President George W. Bush collapses in the White House. He is watching sport on TV and eating a pretzel when he chokes. He faints and hurts his face. His reputation also suffers. This is compounded when the president – known as 'Dubya' – falls off a Segway and rides a bike into a Scottish policeman within a few years.

(Sunday 13 January 2002)

5.40 p.m.

Neville Chamberlain hails the crowd from the steps of his aircraft. The British Prime Minister has returned triumphantly from Munich, after signing an agreement that transfers the Sudeten territory in Czechoslovakia to Hitler's Germany. Chamberlain returns to Downing Street where he says: 'I believe it is peace for our time. Go home and get a nice quiet sleep'. Despite this declaration of peace, extra trains are put on from London to take citizens away to where they feel less likely to be attacked from the air. War is less than a year away.

(Friday 30 September 1938)

5.40 p.m.

Tom Simpson is pronounced dead. The British cyclist has collapsed while attempting an ascent of Mont Ventoux. The 6,200ft-high mountain is part of the Tour de France's stage thirteen. Simpson is dehydrated – the riders are limited to only a certain amount of water – and has also taken amphetamines and alcohol. Nearing the top, he had collapsed but remounted his bike to painfully cycle only a few yards. The next day the other riders allow a British cyclist to win the stage as a tribute.

(Thursday 13 July 1967)

5.45 p.m.

A Messerschmitt Bf 110 aircraft takes off from Augsburg in Germany. The pilot is Hitler's deputy Rudolf Hess. He flies all the way to Britain and then parachutes out of his plane, landing outside Glasgow. His mission is to seek out the Duke of Hamilton in an attempt to end the war. At the post-war Nuremburg trials Hess is jailed for life. He kills himself in 1997, aged 93, having been the only prisoner of Spandau Prison for twenty years.

(Saturday 10 May 1941)

5.59 p.m.

James Dean is dead. The Hollywood movie star's car had collided with another vehicle in Cholame, California. On seeing Dean's Porsche a few days previously, British actor Alec Guinness had told him: 'If you get in that car, you will be found dead in it by this time next week.' Although he has only starred in three movies, Dean becomes an icon of doomed and rebellious youth.

(Friday 30 September 1955)

6.00 P.M. TO 6.59 P.M.

6.00 p.m.

A charred body is found in the basement of the Empire Palace theatre in Edinburgh. The previous night a fire had broken out during a performance by famous American illusionist The Great Lafayette (real name Sigmund Neuburger), which kills ten people. Thought to be that of Charles Richards, a missing member of the company, the body is in fact that of Neuburger. Richards was dressed as Neuburger's body double for the show's finale and his body is prepared to be buried as Neuburger's. The issue is quickly resolved and Neuburger's ashes are buried with his favourite dog 'Beauty' in an Edinburgh cemetery. The dog had died a few days previously and was only allowed to be buried in the cemetery when Neuburger agreed that it would also be his resting place.

(Friday 12 May 1911)

6.00 p.m.

It's closing time at bars in New Zealand. The government has imposed restrictions on alcohol consumption in the name of 'national efficiency', which placates the temperance movement. The move is intended to be temporary during wartime, but the 'six o'clock swill' remains in place for fifty years. Drinkers try to imbibe as much alcohol as possible between the time they leave their work and finishing-up time. In 1967 the closing time is extended to 10 p.m. Similar measures are introduced in Australian states, apart from Western Australia.

(1917–67)

6.00 p.m.

Francis Crick and James Watson go to the pub to discuss the way forward. Earlier that day the Cambridge scientists have discovered the structure of DNA (deoxyribonucleic acid), the molecule that carries genetic information for virtually all organic life. Their discovery of the double helix paves the way for a revolution in criminal investigation, food production, and disease screening, among other applications. Earlier that day Crick had let slip news of their momentous breakthrough by saying in the same pub: 'We have found the secret of life.'

(Saturday 28 February 1953)

6.00 p.m.

The BBC's *Six O'Clock News* bulletin is interrupted by a small group of protestors, who can be heard by viewers. Their protest is about the government's anti-homosexuality Section 28 legislation. Presenter Sue Lawley continues to read the news headlines while co-presenter Nicholas Witchell tackles the intruders, leading to the newspaper headline: 'Beeb man sits on lesbians.'

(Monday 23 May 1988)

6.03 p.m.

Medical student Roger Bannister completes the first mile run in under 4 minutes at the Oxford University running track. 3,000 spectators watch him complete the new world record. Bannister becomes a neurologist and later states that this was of more significance that his achievement on the running track.

(Thursday 6 May 1954)

6.03 p.m.

American civil rights leader Martin Luther King is shot on the balcony of his motel in Memphis, Tennessee. He is taken to hospital but declared dead an hour later. The day before, King had delivered a speech that ended with the words: 'And I've seen the promised land. I may not get there with you. But I want you to know tonight, that we, as a people, will get to the promised land. And I'm happy, tonight. I'm not worried about anything. I'm not fearing any man. Mine eyes have seen the glory of the coming of the Lord.'

(Thursday 4 April 1968)

6.05 p.m.

The ferry *Herald of Free Enterprise* leaves Zeebrugge's inner harbour for Dover. Its bow doors haven't been properly secured and the boat capsizes. Of the 459 on board, 193 passengers and crew are killed. The ferry capsizes in under a minute and a half and if it hadn't come to a halt on a sandbank the death toll would have been higher. It is the worst peacetime maritime disaster involving a British ship since the sinking of the *Titanic*.

(Friday 6 March 1987)

6.22 p.m.

Mark Twain dies. The American author has written some of the best-loved and most enduring American novels, such as *The Adventures of Tom Sawyer* and the sequel *Adventures of Huckleberry Finn*. Curiously, his life is bookended by appearances of Halley's Comet. He is born within two weeks of the comet's perihelion in November 1835. In 1909 he wrote: 'I came in with Halley's Comet in 1835. It's coming again next year and I expect to go out with it.'

(Thursday 21 April 1910)

6.25 p.m.

Counter-terrorism forces arrive on the small Norwegian island of Utøya. They have been sent to investigate reports of gunfire. They find Anders Behring Breivik, a 32-year-old diplomat's son, who immediately surrenders. He has shot dead sixty-nine young people on the island attending a political summer camp. The average age of the victims is 22. It is the world's worst spree killing. Earlier that day he had detonated a fertiliser bomb outside a government building in Oslo, which killed eight people. He explains his actions as coming from a wish to stem the spread of Islam in Europe.

(Friday 22 July 2011)

6.30 p.m.

A memorable concert begins in a Vienna theatre. On a cold winter's night the audience sit through a 4-hour-long performance. It is chaotic at times, with the conductor arguing with the musicians, and one piece has to be restarted. The conductor is the German composer Ludwig van Beethoven. Two new symphonies are premiered, one of them Beethoven's Fifth, now regarded as one of his finest works. It begins with a repetitive motif of four notes in a short-short-short-long sequence that is one of the most well-known in music. This was used during the Second World War to introduce radio broadcasts from Britain to the French Resistance. (The notes mimic the Morse Code letter V – for Victory.) Despite losing his hearing, Beethoven continued to compose and conduct music.

(Thursday 22 December 1808)

6.30 p.m.

Oscar Wilde is arrested in London's Cadogan Hotel. The celebrated Irish author has lost a libel action against the Marquis of Queensberry. The Marquis had left his calling card for Wilde with the words 'posing somdomite' (*sic*) written on it. Wilde is left bankrupt by the action, and then faces criminal charges. He is convicted of 'gross indecency' –

6.30 p.m.: Oscar Wilde is arrested. (Napoleon Sarony)

homosexuality being effectively illegal – and sentenced to two years' hard labour. He dies three years after his release, a broken man. Despite facing financial and emotional hardships in his final years, Wilde retains his famous waspish wit. Remarking on the low-grade Paris hotel in which he is staying, Wilde says: 'My wallpaper and I are fighting a duel to the death. One of us has got to go.'

(Saturday 6 April 1895)

6.30 p.m.

The longest-reigning British monarch dies. Queen Victoria is 81 years old and has been on the throne for sixty-three years. She has reigned over a period of huge social change in Britain and the expansion of the British Empire, on which it was said 'the sun never set'. Victoria had lost her husband Prince Albert in 1861, although it was rumoured that her subsequent relationship with her Scottish ghillie John Brown was more than just a monarch-servant one and they may even have married. Victoria is the last monarch of the House of Hanover. Her son Edward VII is from the House of Saxe-Coburg Gotha, which the Royal Family changes to Windsor during the First World War.

(Tuesday 22 January 1901)

6.30 p.m.

Public transport in the north-east of London has ground almost to a halt. A bank of fog, which has been sitting over the Thames Valley for a number of days, combines with soot and other pollutants from chimneys and vehicle exhausts to form a noxious smog. At times visibility is reported as 'zero'. A performance of the opera *La Traviata* in Sadler's Wells is ended after the first act as the theatre is full of dense fog. It causes widespread transportation disruption and serious health effects, with as many as 12,000 people dying as a result of respiratory and cardiovascular illnesses. It leads to the Clean Air Act being enacted in 1956.

(Tuesday 9 December 1952)

6.30 p.m.

Michael Jackson's hair catches fire. The singer is filming a soft drinks commercial in front of 3,000 fans when a pyrotechnic goes off too close to his head. He continues dancing, unaware that his hair is alight. He suffers severe burns and the incident is later given as a reason for his reliance on painkillers. Jackson was unsure about promoting Pepsi. He is reported to have said beforehand: 'In my heart I feel it's wrong to endorse something you don't believe in. I think it's a bad omen.'

(Friday 27 January 1984)

6.35 p.m.

The wife of Conservative government minister Jonathan Aitken checks in her rental car in Geneva. This later is used as evidence that she couldn't have been in Paris to pay her husband's Ritz Hotel bill at 4.30 p.m. Aitken has been staying in Paris to meet Saudi Arabian officials. They pay his hotel bill, which is against government rules. When allegations are made by the *Guardian* newspaper and Granada TV, Aitken issues a challenge: 'If it falls to me to start a fight to cut out the cancer of bent and twisted journalism in our country with the simple sword of truth and the trusty shield of fair play, so be it.' He is found guilty of perjury and jailed for eighteen months, the first British Cabinet minister to go to jail.

(Sunday 19 September 1993)

6.35 p.m.

While campaigning in Wales for the 2001 General Election, Deputy Prime Minister John Prescott is hit by an egg. He immediately responds with a punch. The assailant, local farm worker Craig Evans, is arrested but later released without charge. Prescott fears having to resign but the incident only adds to his reputation as a no-nonsense politician. New Labour go on to win their second term in power, with a landslide victory over the William Hague-led Conservatives.

(Wednesday 16 May 2001)

6.40 p.m.

Zola Budd collides with Mary Decker in the women's 3,000m Olympic final in Los Angeles. With just over three laps to go, the bare-footed runner had come into contact with Decker several times. Decker, the current world champion, stumbles and falls into the infield. Romania's Maricica Pucia goes on to win gold. Budd finishes seventh. The 18-year-old

South African had already caused controversy after being selected for the British athletics team. Decker is helped from the track by British discuss thrower Richard Slaney, whom she later marries.

(Saturday 1 August 1984)

6.43 p.m.

Mathias Rust lands in Moscow's Red Square. The 19-year-old German has flown to Russia's capital from Helsinki in a Cessna 172 light aircraft. He claims his flight was intended to help ease tensions caused by the Cold War. He is jailed for four years but is released early in 1988. His unauthorised flight causes upheaval in Russia's military hierarchy, who are blamed for allowing a western aircraft to fly all the way to the Russian capital through the country's air defences. Senior figures are relieved of their posts by Mikhail Gorbachev. Rust never flies again.

(Thursday 28 May 1987)

6.45 p.m.

A new radio entertainment programme is broadcast on the BBC. *Crazy People* features radio's own Crazy Gang: the future *Goons* stars Spike Milligan, Peter Sellers, Harry Secombe and Michael Bentine. The show includes short comedy sketches interspersed with musical items. The next year they return with *The Goon Show*, which becomes a landmark in the development of British comedy.

(Monday 28 May 1951)

7.00 P.M. TO 7.59 P.M.

7.00 p.m.

The first episode of *Coronation Street* is broadcast. The show, broadcast live, is seen in 3.5 million homes. It becomes the world's longest-running TV soap opera, with almost 7,500 episodes by its fiftieth anniversary. Jack Duckworth, Ken Barlow and Ena Sharples become household names.

(Friday 9 December 1960)

7.00 p.m.

Archie MacPherson telephones his mother to let her know he is on his way to her house. Waves have been blown by hurricane-strength winds over the top of his house in South Uist in the Outer Hebrides. MacPherson, his wife, their two children and his wife's father are going to drive to higher ground. The two cars set out along the short distance to his mother's house but don't make it. Both cars are found underwater the next day. The tragedy affects the population deeply. A member of the church says about the funeral: 'I didn't think it was possible for an island to break its heart, but it has happened before my own eyes.'

(Wednesday 12 January 2005)

7.02 p.m.

Contact is lost with Boeing 747 airliner N739PA, which is flying at 31,000ft over southern Scotland. An explosion from a bomb in the Pan Am aircraft's hold has caused the plane to break up, and 270 people die as a result, including eleven on the ground in the town of Lockerbie. Although it is thought that most passengers died instantly, one is reportedly found clutching a clump of grass.

(Wednesday 21 December 1988)

7.13 p.m.

A signal is sent to the north end of the Tay Rail Bridge at Dundee that the Edinburgh train is just starting to cross. Shortly afterwards, sparks are seen from underneath the train. Moments later all the lights from the train disappear. The central section of the bridge has collapsed. All the crew and passengers are killed in a disaster that shocks Victorian pride in engineering accomplishment. It is later found that the bridge was not constructed in a manner able to withstand the force 10 gale that was blowing that evening. Poet William McGonagall writes a poem on the event, which ends: 'For the stronger we our houses do build, The less chance we have of being killed.'

(Sunday 28 December 1879)

7.15 p.m.

Celtic win the European Champions Cup. They are the first British club to lift the trophy. The team, all of whom are Scottish and were born within 30 miles of the club's stadium in the east end of Glasgow, have defeated Inter Milan. The Italian club had won the trophy twice before with their controlled, defensive style of football. Over 12,000 Celtic fans made their way to Lisbon to see the game. Legendary Liverpool manager Bill Shankly congratulates Celtic's manager Jock Stein and says: 'John, you're immortal now.' The final is the culmination of a season in which Celtic win every competition they enter.

(Thursday 25 May 1967)

7.23 p.m.

A team of Special Air Service (SAS) soldiers set off explosives as they launch an assault on the Iranian Embassy in London. Gunmen had stormed the building and held hostages there in a siege lasting six days. After one of the hostages is shot dead, the SAS are given orders to start their operation. Five of the six terrorists and one of the hostages are killed in the attack, which is shown live on television, bringing this normally secretive army regiment to international prominence.

(Monday 5 May 1980)

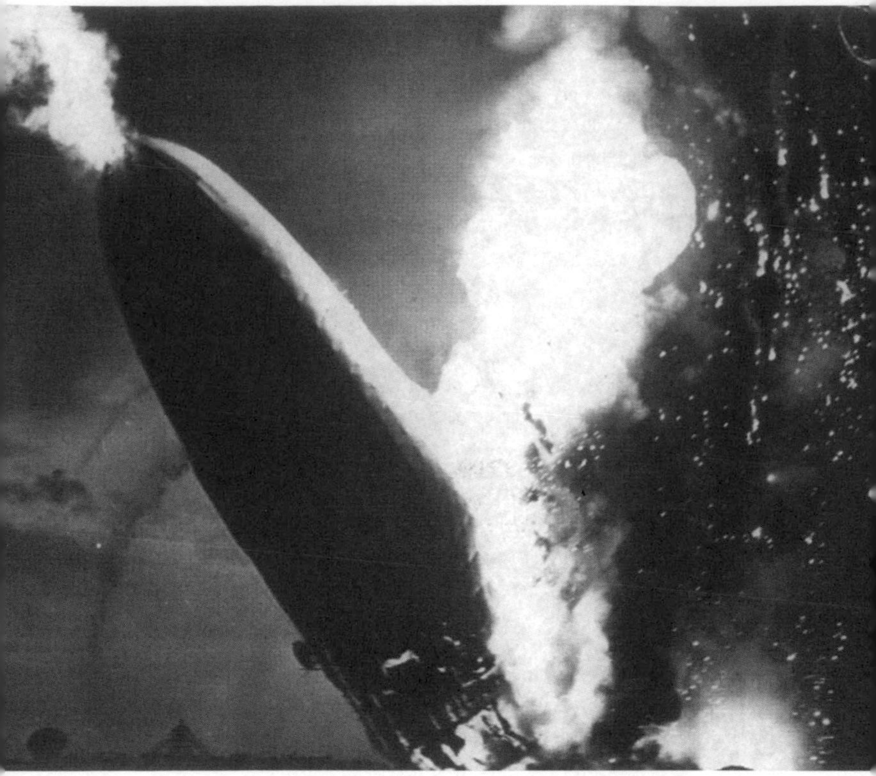

7.25 p.m.: The *Hindenburg* bursts into flames. (National Archives)

7.25 p.m.

The *Hindenburg* catches fire as it comes in to land. The giant German airship is at the end of its first Atlantic crossing of the year at New Jersey's Lakehurst Naval Air Station. As it comes close to the landing area a fire is seen. It soon spreads. The hydrogen-filled airship becomes engulfed in flames, and collapses to the ground, exposing its metal frame. Some of the passengers and crew jump to escape the inferno. Thirty-six people die as a result of the accident. It is caught on film and Herbert Morrison's emotional commentary is broadcast to the whole of America the next day. He finishes his broadcast by saying: 'This is the worst thing I've ever witnessed.'

(Thursday 6 May 1937)

7.25 p.m.

Leon Trotsky dies. The former senior figure in the Russian Communist government had been attacked and mortally wounded by a Spanish communist in his own home the previous day. His assailant used an ice axe. Trotksy had been ousted from power by Stalin following Lenin's death and had been exiled to Mexico. He had been war commissar and organised the formation of the Red Army.

(Wednesday 21 August 1940)

7.30 p.m.

A murder mystery play opens in London's West End, starring Richard Attenborough and Sylvia Sim. It is Agatha Christie's *The Mousetrap*. The play becomes the longest-running production in the world with over 24,000 performances by 2011. After each performance the audience are asked not to reveal the surprise ending.

(Tuesday 25 November 1952)

7.30 p.m.

Elvis Presley arrives in Britain. For the first and only time, 'The King' steps onto British soil at Prestwick Airport. He is flying back to America after military service in Germany and has only a couple of hours on the ground. He is reported to have asked: 'Where am I?'

(Thursday 3 March 1960)

7.30 p.m.

The first Earth Hour starts. Designed to raise awareness of climate change, householders, businesses and organisations are asked to switch off any unnecessary electrical appliances or lights. The first one is held in Sydney, Australia, but it quickly becomes a global event.

(Saturday 31 March 2007)

7.35 p.m.

Barack Obama is sworn in as President of the United States – for the second time. There was a mix-up with the exact wording during the public inauguration the previous day. A spokesman says an 'abundance of caution' explains why the oath was retaken by the president, who is the first black person to be elected to the White House.

(Wednesday 21 January 2009)

7.40 p.m.

The Grand Knockout Tournament begins on BBC One. Organised by Prince Edward, the programme is a special edition of *It's a Knockout* featuring members of the British Royal Family such as Princess Anne, Prince Andrew and his wife Sarah Ferguson. Despite raising money for charity, the show is much criticised. Prince Edward is unimpressed by the press's immediate reaction, saying: 'Thanks for sounding so bloody enthusiastic', before leaving a press conference. The broadcast gets an audience of 18 million but some commentators believe the show has damaged royalty irretrievably.

(Friday 19 June 1987)

7.42 p.m.

A train leaves Slough for London's Paddington station. A telegraph is sent to Paddington: 'A murder has gust been committed at Salt Hill and the suspected murderer was seen to take a first class ticket to London by the train which left Slough at 7.42pm. He is in the garb of a Kwaker with a great coat on which reaches nearly down to his feet. He is in the last compartment of the second class compartment' (the keys Q, Z and J are not available on this system). The man is John Tawell, a Quaker, who is followed by a policeman at Paddington and later arrested and then hanged for the murder of his mistress. The incident serves as an example of the usefulness of the new electric telegraph method of communication, which has just been installed on part of the Great Western Railway.

(Wednesday 1 January 1845)

7.45 p.m.

Vincent Van Gogh's 'Portrait of Dr Gachet' is auctioned in New York. It fetches a world-record price for an artwork at that time: $75 million. It is bought by a Japanese businessman called Ryoei Saito, who earns criticism later for saying he wishes to be buried with the work. He dies in 1996, and since then the painting has not been seen publicly.

(Tuesday 15 May 1990)

8.00 P.M. TO 8.59 P.M.

8.00 p.m.

Charles Dickens gives his last public reading. At London's St James' Hall, in front of an audience of 2,000, he reads from *A Christmas Carol* and *The Pickwick Papers*. Dickens is the foremost author of his day, having written popular works such as *Oliver Twist*, *David Copperfield*, *Great Expectations* and *A Tale of Two Cities*. As well as his literary work, Dickens campaigns on liberal issues such as slavery and capital punishment. At the end of his final performance he says: 'From these garish lights I vanish now for evermore'. He dies three months later and is buried in Westminster Abbey.

(Tuesday 15 March 1870)

8.00 p.m.

An American radio dramatisation of H.G. Wells' *War of the Worlds* goes on the air. Narrated by Orson Welles, the production causes panic and anxiety for some listeners, fooled by the authentic nature of the show which uses fake 'on the spot' news broadcasts to tell of an invasion from Mars. Most listeners have tuned in late, missing the introduction announcing that it is just a radio play. Welles moves to Hollywood and directs one of cinema's greatest films: *Citizen Kane*.

(Sunday 30 October 1938)

8.00 p.m.

A plane carrying Egyptian President Anwar Sadat touches down in Jerusalem. He receives a warm welcome, although some Israelis believe his historic visit is just a cover for another surprise attack, similar to the 1973 Yom Kippur conflict. On meeting an Israeli general, Sadat says: 'You see, I wasn't bluffing.' Sadat is the first Arab leader to recognise the state of Israel and the first to visit it. Following the signing of the peace treaty between Egypt and Israel in 1979 he is awarded the Nobel Peace Prize. His efforts to bring peace to the region are not always popular and Sadat is shot dead in 1981, on the eighth anniversary of the Yom Kippur war.

(Saturday 19 November 1977)

8.00 p.m.

Gordon Brown is due to meet Tony Blair for dinner at a London restaurant called Granita's. Their meeting is one in a series where the two MPs discuss who will succeed Labour leader John Smith, who had died of a heart attack a few weeks previously. Brown agrees not to stand and in return Blair gives the shadow chancellor freedom in domestic policy. Over the years, their once-close relationship descends into barely disguised enmity, as Brown believes Blair has reneged on an agreement to stand down from the position of prime minister earlier than he does.

(Tuesday 31 May 1994)

8.00 p.m.

The Time Traveller Convention starts on the American Massachusetts Institute of Technology campus. It is organised by students and features music, speeches and a DeLorean car. The organisation notes state: 'Time travellers can come at 8 pm or 10 pm.' No confirmed time travellers make their presence known, although the event organisers understand that some may have remained incognito to avoid being pestered with questions about the future.

(Saturday 7 May 2005)

8.05 p.m.

A man gets off a bus in the San Fernando district of Buenos Aires. He is identified and pulled into a car. He is ex-SS senior officer Adolf Eichmann, and his kidnappers are Israeli Mossad agents. They smuggle their prisoner to Israel where he is put on trial for war crimes and crimes against humanity. Despite claiming that he was only following orders Eichmann is hanged for his role in supervising the transportation of Jews to concentration camps.

(Wednesday 11 May 1960)

8.13 p.m.

The crew of a hijacked airliner notice the aircraft's rear passenger steps have been deployed. When the Boeing 727 lands at Reno Airport 2 hours later the hijacker is gone. Just after the initial take-off a passenger who gave his name as Dan Cooper told a stewardess that he had a bomb and then issued a set of demands. He wanted four parachutes, $200,000 and for the plane to fly to Mexico. 'Dan Cooper' is never found, although some of the money is recovered several years later.

(Wednesday 24 November 1971)

8.17 p.m.

The *Eagle* lands. The lunar module, piloted by Neil Armstrong and Buzz Aldrin, touches down in the Sea of Tranquility. The historic landing is

8.17 p.m.: Man lands on the moon. (NASA)

watched by hundreds of millions back on Earth. Six and a half hours later Armstrong descends the spacecraft's ladder to take the first walk on the moon. As he steps off the landing pad he utters one of the most famous of phrases: 'That's one small step for [a] man, one giant leap for mankind.' Shortly afterwards, Aldrin joins him on the surface and describes the landscape in front of him as 'magnificent desolation'. Both men return safely to Earth with fellow *Apollo 11* astronaut Michael Collins four days later.

(Sunday 20 July 1969)

8.25 p.m.

A missile hits the aircraft carrying Rwandan President Juvénal Habyarimana. His death is the spark that starts a period of genocide in the country. The majority Hutus carry out an organised programme of rape and murder against the Tutsis and some moderate Hutus, that lasts for 100 days. It is estimated that over 1 million die – a sixth of the population. Many are killed with machetes.

(Wednesday 6 April 1994)

8.30 p.m.

An edition of the BBC's *Panorama* current affairs programme includes a report on the Swiss spaghetti harvest. It explains how the spaghetti grows at a standard length and how the 'spaghetti weevil' can affect the crop. The April Fool's Day prank gets a mixed reaction, with some not seeing the funny side of Richard Dimbleby's broadcast on a normally serious show.

(Monday 1 April 1957)

8.30 p.m.

Armed men enter the stud farm where Shergar the racehorse is being kept. Shergar had been put out to stud in Ireland after a successful racing career. He is kidnapped by the IRA, and after ransom demands are not met, is machine-gunned to death. Shergar's remains are never found. The police chief superintendent leading the search says: 'A clue? That is something we haven't got.'

(Tuesday 8 February 1983)

8.30 p.m.

Comedian and magician Tommy Cooper collapses live on television. Performing at a London theatre he suffers a fatal heart attack in front of millions. At first the audience think his fall is part of the act. He dies before reaching hospital.

(Sunday 15 April 1984)

8.36 p.m.

Saddam Hussein is captured by US troops who find him hiding in a small underground chamber. When captured he says: 'My name is Saddam Hussein. I am the president of Iraq and I want to negotiate.' The former dictator is found guilty of crimes against humanity and is hanged three years later.

(Saturday 13 December 2003)

8.40 p.m.

Clydebank's air raid sirens go off for the second night running. The first night's raids have brought devastation to the Clydeside town. The Luftwaffe target shipyards and factories but hit residential areas. Official figures put the death toll at 528, although many believe it is much higher. Out of the 12,000 homes in the town less than ten are undamaged after two nights of bombing. Almost 50,000 people are made homeless following the attacks. The raids are not fully reported in the press, with one national paper describing damage and casualties as 'remarkably light'.

(Friday 14 March 1941)

8.45 p.m.

Ronnie Kray claims that he is in the Widow's pub in London's East End at this time, when he hears news of the murder of a man called George Cornell. Kray goes on trial at the Old Bailey for the murder, which was committed in a different pub – the Blind Beggar – between 8 p.m. and 9 p.m. that night. A barmaid testifies that Kray came into the bar and shot Cornell through the forehead, in full view of other customers. Kray's twin brother Reggie is also on trial, for the murder of Jack 'the Hat' McVitie. The Krays are the heads of a criminal gang known as 'The Firm'. Both are given life imprisonment sentences.

(Wednesday 9 March 1966)

8.58 p.m.

Arriving at Plymouth harbour, yachtsman Francis Chichester completes his solo circumnavigation of the world. The 65-year-old is the first to go round the world by the 'clipper' route single-handed. His epic journey has taken nine months and one day, and included only one stop, in Australia. He is knighted by the same sword used to honour Sir Francis Drake.

(Sunday 28 May 1967)

9.00 P.M. TO 9.59 P.M.

9.00 p.m.

Michael Faraday begins the first 'Friday Evening Discourse' at the Royal Institution. His lecture on a natural form of rubber begins a programme aiming to popularise the teaching of science. Faraday also introduces the popular 'Christmas Lectures' series for young people, which continues to the present day. Faraday is one of science's foremost figures, having produced the first electric motor and the first transformer and generator. He helps to improve the effectiveness of lighthouses, for which he is gifted a house in Hampton Court by a grateful nation.

(Friday 3 February 1826)

9.00 p.m.

George Loveless is placed in the *York* hulk prison ship at Portsmouth. Along with five other men he has been sentenced to transportation to Australia for taking an illegal oath after organising to protest against reduced wages. The men are described in contemporary reports as the 'Dorchester labourers' but become known as the 'Tolpuddle Martyrs'. Petitions and a march through London are organised as part of a campaign to reverse their 'cruel and oppressive' punishment, which eventually succeeds, and in 1837 Loveless is the first to return to the United Kingdom. Five of the six immigrate to Canada to begin new lives.

(Saturday 5 April 1834)

9.05 p.m.

'Cathy Come Home' is broadcast. This 75 minute-long episode of the BBC series *The Wednesday Play* has a huge influence on the issue of homelessness in Britain. The drama sees a couple's children taken away into care in emotional scenes made more powerful by Ken Loach's documentary style of film-making. The programme focuses attention on the issue and helps the recently formed homeless charity Shelter.

(Wednesday 16 November 1966)

9.05 p.m.

Gerry McCann checks on his children in their Portuguese holiday apartment. He sees all three and makes his way back to the restaurant where his wife and friends are. It's the last time he sees his 3-year-old daughter Madeleine, whose disappearance becomes the focus of a campaign intensified by heavy media coverage. Despite numerous reported sightings and investigative leads, she remains missing.

(Thursday 3 May 2007)

9.15 p.m.

The TV show *Britain's Got Talent* ends and a star is born. The Scottish singer Susan Boyle becomes a worldwide sensation following her version of 'I Dreamed a Dream'. Her performance is viewed millions of times on

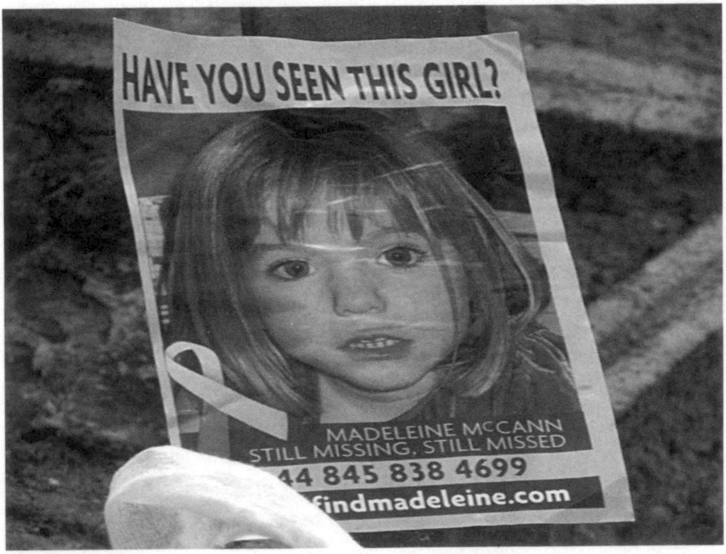

9.05 p.m.: Madeleine McCann is seen for the last time. (Waerfelu)

the Internet and her dream of becoming a professional singer becomes reality. In only six weeks her debut album sells 9 million copies.

(Saturday 11 April 2009)

9.30 p.m.

Mary Byrne leaves the vicinity of Knock parish church. She, along with many others, has seen three figures outside the church. Mary understands the apparitions to be the Virgin Mary, her husband Joseph and St John the Evangelist. They float in front of a plain altar on which is set a lamb. The visions result in millions making pilgrimages to the small Irish town. Monsignor Horan, the parish priest, oversees the building of a new basilica and encourages the construction of a new airport. While on a visit to London in 1986 he dies and his coffin is the first to be flown into the airport.

(Thursday 21 August 1879)

9.30 p.m.

Secondo Pia begins photographing the shroud in Turin's Cathedral of St John. Later that night, Pia develops his images and almost drops the glass plate in astonishment. He writes: 'Alone, I witnessed a strong sensation when I saw for the first time, the Holy Face.' His negative reveals an image of a bearded man that causes a sensation. The shroud, which is later carbon dated to the thirteenth or fourteenth centuries, is the subject of much debate as to whether it is the actual cloth in which Jesus' body was wrapped after his crucifixion, or a medieval forgery.

(Friday 28 May 1898)

9.30 p.m.

Three prisoners make their first moves to escape from the island prison Alcatraz. Frank Morris and brothers John and Clarence Anglin have spent months preparing for their break out. Their plan is to use life rafts made from raincoats. They make it out into the San Francisco Bay waters and are never seen again. It is assumed that they all drown, although there are claims that they have survived. Alcatraz is a notorious prison, situated 1.5 miles off San Francisco's shore. The isolation felt by the prisoners is worsened when, with the right wind conditions, they can hear the noise from bars in the city.

(Monday 11 June 1962)

9.30 p.m.

Guo Bing Long telephones his family to tell them that he is trapped in the sea. He is one of a group of Chinese cockle pickers working in Morecambe Bay. Twenty-three are swept away by the incoming tide and drown. The workers are illegal immigrants employed by a gang master, who is later jailed for manslaughter. One of the victims' bodies is not found.

(Thursday 5 February 2004)

9.41 p.m.

A light aircraft piloted by John F. Kennedy Jr crashes into the sea off Martha's Vineyard, Massachusetts. The son of the late president is killed, along with his wife and sister-in-law. He is not qualified to fly on instruments. John F. Kennedy Jr was only 2 years old when his father was assassinated, and images of him saluting his father's coffin touch those watching.

(Friday 16 July 1999)

9.42 p.m.

Eva Peron's death is announced. She had risen to international prominence as the husband of Juan Peron, who became President of Argentina in 1946. Known as 'Evita' she was revered by the poor and the working class, and was seen as their champion, although the ruling elite did not view her with the same warmth. When she died huge crowds gathered outside the Ministry of Labour to see her lying in state. Some were injured or even killed in the crush. Juan Peron had his wife embalmed so that people could pay their respects for years to come.

(Saturday 26 July 1952)

9.45 p.m.

Fire breaks out in the Reichstag, Germany's parliament. Hitler's rule tightens on the Fatherland after he blames the fire on the communists. He is able to pass legislation passing power to himself as chancellor. Hitler exerts a powerful hold on German society and leads it into an expansionism that ultimately fails, ending in defeat in 1945.

(Monday 27 February 1933)

9.45 p.m.

A blood-stained woman bursts into a London pub claiming her husband has attacked her and killed their children's nanny. The woman is Lady Lucan and within a few hours her estranged husband Lord Lucan disappears. His whereabouts become a long-running mystery that, despite numerous reported sightings, is never solved.

(Thursday 7 November 1974)

9.50 p.m.

Magician David Blaine comes down to earth for the first time in forty-four days. The American has spent his time suspended in a clear plastic box 400ft above London. During his fasting endurance test he has lost 50lbs in weight and was subjected to taunting from onlookers below. One flies fast food up towards him on a remote-controlled helicopter. Some have also distracted him by flashing their breasts (women) and buttocks (men).

(Sunday 19 October 2003)

9.57 p.m.

The three astronauts of *Apollo 8* make a memorable television broadcast. Frank Borman, Jim Lovell and Bill Anders all take turns to read from the opening passages of Genesis as they orbit the Moon. They are the first humans to reach earth's nearest neighbour. The commander of the flight, Frank Borman, ends the broadcast: 'And from the crew of Apollo 8, we close with good night, good luck, a Merry Christmas and God bless all of you – all of you on the good Earth.'

(Tuesday 24 December 1968)

10.00 P.M. TO 10.59 P.M.

10.00 p.m.

The alarm is given on the schooner *Black Joke*, anchored off the Chinese island of Lantao. Chinese men board the ship and murder most of the crew. The only passenger is Briton Mark Moss, who is beaten unconscious and has his ear cut off and put into his throat to kill him. The incident is a sign of the rising tension that leads to the Opium Wars. Britain's keenness to continue the lucrative drug trade is not appreciated by the Chinese, who see its destructive social and economic effects. The wars lead to concessions benefitting British trade and territory such as Hong Kong being transferred to British authority, giving the Empire a commercial base in the Far East.

(Saturday 24 August 1839)

10.00 p.m.

John Wilkes Booth shoots Abraham Lincoln as the president watches a play in Washington's Ford's Theatre. The assassin is hoping the shooting and his fellow conspirators' actions will spark a resurgence in the South's fight against the Union. The attack on Lincoln comes five days after the Confederate General Robert E. Lee surrenders. Lincoln dies the next morning, the first US president to be assassinated.

(Friday 14 April 1865)

10.00 p.m.

Dancer Isadora Duncan is being driven to her hotel in Nice in the south of France. The dancer is wearing a long scarf, the ends of which become entangled in the spokes of the open-topped car's wheels. She is dragged out onto the road and dies instantly of strangulation and a broken neck.

10.00 p.m.: US president Abraham Lincoln is shot. (Alexander Gardner)

Famous for her free-flowing dancing, she is credited with the invention of modern dance.

(Wednesday 14 September 1927)

10.00 p.m.

An explosion on the production deck of oil platform *Piper Alpha* starts a fire that soon spreads to the rest of the structure. Only sixty-one workers survive out of the 226 on board. Some escape by jumping from the 175ft-high helicopter deck into the sea. The accident is the worst in the history of North Sea oil exploration.

(Monday 6 July 1988)

10.08 p.m.

Astronaut Jack Swigert transmits a terse message to Mission Control. While performing a routine function on his spacecraft's oxygen tanks he says: 'Okay Houston, we've had a problem here.' Fifty-five hours into its flight to the moon *Apollo 13* faces a loss in its power and oxygen supplies. The crew and ground staff work to overcome the problems. The crew return to Earth safely four days later. None return to the Moon.

(Monday 13 April 1970)

10.08 p.m.

Asteroid 2004 FH makes the closest ever recorded pass by Earth. The 100ft-diameter rock passes within the Moon's orbit, at a distance of 26,500 miles from Earth. The asteroid is picked up by the Lincoln Near-Earth Asteroid Program, set up to detect objects approaching our planet. This time there is no risk to humankind.

(Thursday 18 March 2004)

10.10 p.m.

Barings Bank goes into administration, with losses of £860 million. Britain's oldest merchant bank has been brought to a state of collapse due to the disastrous trading of Nick Leeson. Leeson, based in Singapore, had exposed the bank through deception and attempting to win back his trading losses. He had gone on the run, leaving behind a note saying: 'I'm sorry.'

(Sunday 26 February 1995)

10.20 p.m.

Hitler's death is announced on German radio: 'Hitler has fallen this afternoon at his command post in the Reich Chancery fighting to the last breath against Bolshevism and for Germany.' In reality he has shot himself and his recently wed wife Eva Braun has taken cyanide. Their bodies are burnt by staff. Hitler's remains are eventually crushed by the Russians and thrown into a river, to avoid his grave becoming a Nazi shrine.

(Tuesday 1 May 1945)

10.25 p.m.

The light entertainment show *BBC-3* begins on BBC One. It includes an appearance by theatre critic Kenneth Tynan. During a discussion on censorship he utters the first recorded use of the f-word. It results in a storm of protest with television campaigner Mary Whitehouse writing to the queen to request that she use her influence with the BBC governors to prevent it happening again. The BBC state: 'We had no knowledge that Mr Tynan was going to say this.'

(Saturday 13 November 1965)

10.28 p.m.

Russia's *Sputnik 1* is launched into space, becoming the world's first satellite. Its arrival provokes fears from the West that Russia now has a military advantage. It spurs America to respond, leading to the Space Race. The aluminium sphere emits a simple bleeping signal for three months before burning up in Earth's atmosphere.

(Friday 4 October 1957)

10.30 p.m.

Leonardo da Vinci is born. During his life the Italian produces a body of work in different disciplines that ensures he is regarded as one of the greatest minds in human civilisation. He is known for his skills in drawing and painting, with works such as 'The Last Supper', 'Mona Lisa' and the 'Vitruvian Man'. As an engineer he draws up plans for town defences and bridges. Leonardo devises many innovations, including a helicopter, five centuries before the first one would fly.

(Saturday 15 April 1452)

10.30 p.m.

Princess Grace of Monaco dies in hospital. The former Hollywood actress had been involved in a car accident two days previously. The princess and her daughter Stephanie were travelling on a mountain road when their car fell 100ft down a ravine. At her funeral, Britain is represented by Princess Diana.

(Tuesday 14 September 1982)

10.30 p.m.

A gate is ordered open at one of East Berlin's checkpoints. East Berliners rush through to the west, some for the first time. It is estimated that 100,000 cross the border overnight. Celebrations continue with attempts to knock down the wall that has encircled the city for almost thirty years. It is the most visible sign of the end of the Cold War.

(Thursday 9 November 1989)

10.40 p.m.

The Soviet flag is raised over Berlin's Reichstag. The Red Army have entered the German capital and have fought their way to the building seen as the symbolic heart of Nazi rule, despite being unused since 1933. The raising of the flag is staged again a few days later for the benefit of propaganda photographer Yevgeny Khaldei, who takes one of the iconic images of the Second World War, deliberately mimicking a similar American photograph taken at Iwo Jima.

(Monday 30 April 1945)

10.40 p.m.

The Sun newspaper rolls off the presses for the first time. It is initially a broadsheet but following its acquisition by Rupert Murdoch it is re-launched as a tabloid and includes nude photographs of women on page 3. *The Sun* gains a reputation for salacious stories and achieves notoriety for its 'Gotcha' headline following the sinking of the *Belgrano* in 1982. The paper is the subject of a boycott by Liverpudlians after it publishes false stories suggesting fans urinated on policemen and stole from victims at the Hillsborough football disaster.

(Tuesday 15 September 1964)

10.45 p.m.

A dance floor collapses during a wedding reception in Jerusalem. Twenty-three people are killed and 356 guests and staff are injured as the top floor of the Versailles banquet hall gives way. It is Israel's worst civilian disaster and the owners of the hall and some of those responsible for its construction are later found guilty on negligence charges.

(Thursday 24 May 2001)

10.50 p.m.

Morgan Earp is shot dead while playing billiards. He is one of the Earp brothers who, along with Doc Holliday, took part in one of the most famous of gunfights, that near the OK Corral. The shootout in Tombstone, Arizona, only lasted 30 seconds, but gained a special place in the history of the Wild West. The Earps and Holliday are caught up in controversy over who fired first and whether some of the Clanton gang were unarmed.

(Saturday 18 March 1882)

10.50 p.m.

John Lennon is shot outside his apartment in New York. The 40-year-old ex-Beatle is pronounced dead in hospital less than 20 minutes later. His wife Yoko Ono was with him during the shooting. Lennon had recently returned to public life with the release of his album *Double Fantasy*. He had written some of popular music's most enduring and memorable songs both with The Beatles and as a solo artist. One of the songs on his newest album is entitled 'Starting Over'.

(Monday 8 December 1980)

11.00 P.M. TO MIDNIGHT

11.00 p.m.

Nicolas Copernicus sees the star Aldebaran being occluded by the unlit part of the Moon. This astronomical observation helps him to construct a new theory of the heavens. He proposes that the Sun remains still and the planets, including Earth, rotate around it. His heliocentric view of the solar system has no initial repercussions but causes problems for later astronomers such as Galileo. Copernicus' book containing his theory: *De revolutionibus orbium coelestium libri vi* (Six Books Concerning the Revolutions of the Heavenly Orbs) is published just before his death. Legend has it that a copy is placed in his hands shortly before he dies.

(Thursday 9 March 1497)

11.00 p.m.

The BBC makes its first regular television broadcast. Using Scottish inventor John Logie Baird's electromechanical system, the half-hour programme is listed as: 'Television transmission by the Baird Process (Vision): Introduction by John L Baird. The programme: Betty Bolton, Fred Douglas, Betty Astell, and Louie Freear'. The BBC later decides to adopt Marconi-EMI's all-electronic system.

(Monday 22 August 1932)

11.15 p.m.

Edward Kennedy and former Kennedy assistant Mary Jo Kopechne leave a party on the island of Chappaquiddick near Martha's Vineyard in Massachusetts. The US Senator is driving when the car leaves the road while crossing a wooden bridge. The car overturns and sinks, and, while Kennedy is able to swim clear, his passenger drowns. Kennedy is given a suspended jail sentence for abandoning the scene of a crime. The scandal prevents any successful attempt on the presidency by the brother of John and Robert Kennedy.

(Saturday 18 July 1969)

11.15 p.m.

The final frame of the World Championship snooker final begins. Dennis Taylor has come back from being 8-0 down to Steve Davis and the match is now level at seventeen frames each. Taylor builds a twenty-point lead then Davis overcomes it to lead by eighteen with twenty-two points on the table. Taylor gets to within three points of Davis by sinking the blue and pink. Both players manage to miss the black – the final ball of the tournament – five times. After midnight, Taylor finally puts it away to win. Over 18 million watch the tense match come to a dramatic end.

(Sunday 28 April 1985)

11.16 p.m.

A radio telescope at the Big Ear observatory in Ohio picks up a signal that can't be explained. The volunteer astronomer Dr Jerry R. Ehman notices the signal on a computer printout a few days later and writes 'Wow!' in the margin. The signal is analysed and debated over but its origins, whether terrestrial or extraterrestrial, remain unknown.

(Monday 15 August 1977)

11.30 p.m.

Vincent Van Gogh presents a gift to a prostitute in an Arles brothel. It is part of his left ear, which he has cut off with a razor. The Dutch artist suffers dreadful hallucinations and periods of hyperactivity and depression, which suggest that he was bipolar. In July 1890 he shoots himself and dies a few days later. He is only 37 and at the peak of his creative powers. In ten years he produced 900 paintings. In one of his last letters to his brother Theo he writes: 'There are vast stretches of corn under troubled skies, and I did not have to go out of my way very much in order to try to express sadness and extreme loneliness.'

(Sunday 23 December 1888)

11.38 p.m.

A limpet mine explodes on the *Rainbow Warrior*. The Greenpeace ship is in dock in New Zealand when it is sabotaged by French government agents. A second mine goes off minutes later and the ship keels over. A member of the crew, a Portuguese photographer, is drowned. The ship was on its way to protest against French nuclear tests.

(Wednesday 10 July 1985)

11.40 p.m.

Despite urgent efforts to turn away, the RMS *Titanic* hits an iceberg. At the time of the collision the ship is travelling at the fastest speed it has achieved during its maiden transatlantic journey: 21 knots. Within 3 hours the liner sinks. The forward section goes under first, lifting the rest of the ship out of the water, breaking it in two. Passengers who are unable to escape cling to the ship's deck as it rises. It reaches an angle of 70 degrees before sliding under the water. There are insufficient lifeboats. Of all on board only a third are saved. Of the survivors, 60 per cent are first-class passengers. Only a quarter of third class passengers reach their destination alive.

(Sunday 14 April 1912)

11.40 p.m.: RMS *Titanic* hits an iceberg. (National Archives)

11.46 p.m.

The *Voyager I* unmanned spacecraft makes its closest approach to Saturn. Once its primary mission is accomplished, it heads out of the solar system. In December 2010, 10.8 billion miles from the Sun and thirty-three years since it left Earth, it sends signals home that it can no longer detect the Sun's solar wind, indicating that it is on the verge of reaching interstellar space. Travelling at its current rate of 38,000mph, it will take 70,000 years to reach the Solar System's nearest star, Proxima Centauri.

(Wednesday 12 November 1980)

11.47 p.m.

Louise Joy Brown comes into the world. Weighing 5lbs 12oz, she is the first ever 'test tube baby'. The IVF process sees a revolution in human reproduction, with eggs able to be fertilised outside the mother's body. Louise had grown for two and a half days before being placed inside her mother's womb.

(Tuesday 25 July 1978)

11.53 p.m.

The Doomsday Clock starts, at 7 minutes to midnight. Set up by scientists involved in the Manhattan Project to develop America's atomic bomb, the symbolic clock face reflects how close to extinction humans are, with midnight representing self-inflicted apocalyptic destruction. The clock reaches its latest hour in 1953 when it reaches 11.58 due to the proximity of the USA and USSR testing nuclear weapons. Factors affecting the clock's position are nuclear arms, climate change and bioengineering.

(June 1947)